ESSENTI

Cyprus: Regions and Best places to see

Original text by Robert Bulmer
Updated by George McDonald

© Automobile Association Developments Limited 2007
First published 2007

ISBN-10: 0-7495-4951-3
ISBN-13: 978-0-7495-4951-0

Published by AA Publishing, a trading name of Automobile Association Developments
Limited, whose registered office is Fanum House, Basing View, Basingstoke,
Hampshire RG21 4EA.
Registered number 1878835.

A CIP catalogue record for this book is available from the British Library

Colour separation: MRM Graphics Ltd
Printed and bound in Italy by Printer Trento S.r.l.

A02694
Maps in this title produced from mapping © Freytag-Berndt u. Artaria KG,
1231 Vienna-Austria

About this book

This book is divided into five sections.

The essence of Cyprus pages 6–19
Introduction; Features; Food and Drink; Short Break including the 10 Essentials

Planning pages 20–33
Before You Go; Getting There; Getting Around; Being There

Best places to see pages 34–55
The unmissable highlights of any visit to Cyprus

Best things to do pages 56–81
Great places to have lunch; activities; beaches; places to take the children; off the beaten track; best views and more

Exploring pages 82–161
The best places to visit in Cyprus, organized by area

Maps All map references are to the maps on the covers. For example, Nicosia has the reference 🔢 16J – indicating the grid square in which it can be found.

Prices An indication of the cost of restaurants and cafés at attractions is given by **£** signs: **£££** denotes higher prices, **££** average prices, **£** lower prices.

Hotel prices Room per night (Republic of Cyprus/North Cyprus): **£** budget (under CY£40/YTL109); **££** moderate (CY£40–80/YTL109–218); **£££** expensive to luxury (over CY£80/YTL218).

Restaurant prices A 3-course meal per person without drinks (Republic of Cyprus/North Cyprus): **£** budget (under CY£7/YTL19); **££** moderate (CY£7–14/YTL19–38); **£££** expensive (over CY£14/YTL38).

Contents

BEST THINGS TO DO

EXPLORING...

56 – 81   82 – 187

The essence of...

Cyprus is a land of contour and light – hills, valleys and plains. There are beaches, although not endless sands. The heat of summer robs the land of life: winter rains restore spectacular colour. With its archaeological wonders Cyprus is certainly the stuff of tourist books.

But what of the less tangible Cyprus? There is the interesting first journey to the hotel, with screeching brakes and tyres. Less disconcerting are the marvellous alfresco gastronomic events under awnings at lunch-time and the stars at night. Walks through the pine forests of the high mountains, with their spectacular views, will long be remembered.

THE ESSENCE OF CYPRUS

features

Cyprus, within sight of Asia Minor, is halfway to the Orient, yet it looks more and more to the west. The majority of its visitors are from Europe and in 2004 it joined the European Union. English is spoken island-wide, a legacy of British colonial rule. Nevertheless, in many respects Cyprus remains different and retains its own culture. This complex mixture stems from its location and history. Over the centuries Cyprus has been controlled by most great Mediterranean powers and its people have a diverse, if not exotic, ancestry.

The separation of the island today is an indirect consequence of the arrival of the Ottoman Turks in the 16th century. It is not a division easily ignored – United Nations soldiers and Greek and Turkish flags are everywhere along the Green Line. Nevertheless few visitors dwell on the political situation. Understandably they have other distractions.

GEOGRAPHY

● The island has two significant mountain ranges. Troodos in the centre reaches 1,951m (6,399ft), high enough to ensure snow cover in winter; the Pentadaktylos (Beşparmak) Mountains at 1,046m (3,431ft), are in the Turkish controlled district.

● There are approximately 3,350 hours of sunshine a year, with little chance of rain between May and October.

● The sheep cope with the shortage of grazing in the dry summer by storing fat in their tails.

POPULATION

● The first sign of human habitation dates from 11,000 years ago.

● The island's population is estimated at 985,000, of whom about 640,000 are Greek Cypriots, 180,000 Turkish Cypriots, 8,000 Armenians and Maronites, the rest foreign residents.

● Cypriots have the highest marriage rate in Europe.

ECONOMIC FACTORS

● Forty-six per cent of the land area is cultivated; the main crops are cereals, potatoes and citrus fruits.

● Cyprus has the third-highest standard of living in the Mediterranean. The average income here is twice as high as it is in Greece.

● Cyprus has suffered water shortages because of dry winters. As a result, three desalination plants have been constructed off the south coast and a fourth off the east, providing 120,000cu m (26.4 million gallons) of water per day.

TOURISM

● The island attracts about 2.75 million visitors a year and tourism provides employment for around 40,000 people or 15 per cent of the work force, many of them immigrants.

food & drink

Cyprus has plenty of fresh produce and meat and visitors should take the opportunity to make the most of the fruits that are so plentiful in the summer months. Quite apart from the well-known crops of citrus fruits, there are peaches, plums, cherries, melons and bananas – all readily available in season. Water melons and other fruits are often sold from roadside stalls.

GREEK CUISINE

The old staples of Greek cuisine – moussaka, *stifado*, kebab and Greek salad – will be much in evidence. The *meze* is perhaps a good way to get an insight into Cypriot food. *Meze*, or *mezedhes*, is a series of small different dishes that are provided throughout an evening, and may cover absolutely everything or pursue a fish or a meat theme. In a good restaurant the *meze* can contain up to 30 different dishes and it is important to pace yourself through the meal.

Kebab *(souvlaki)* appears on all menus and lamb is another common dish, either lamb chops or the more traditional *kleftiko*, which consists of large

pieces of lamb baked slowly in traditional *kleftiko* ovens. Cypriots also have a taste for smoked meats, most notably the traditional *loukanika* sausage.

Fish is expensive, although *kalamari* – squid cooked in batter – is good value and widely available. Other fish options include swordfish, red mullet (*barbouni* in Greek), whitebait and sea bass. Alternatively, fresh farmed trout is on the menu in some of the mountain villages.

Halloumi cheese is the main dairy product distinctive to the island. It is made from goat's milk and is often served grilled. The cheese is now available in most supermarkets.

Visitors should seek out some of the cake shops that attract local custom. The traditional Greek desserts such as *baklava* and *cadefi* may be too sweet for some tastes, but the wide range of custard-based cakes should appeal to all, as will the biscuits, which can be bought by weight in these shops.

A similar range of food is available in the Turkish part of the island. Some dishes such as *sis kebab* and *cacik* (cucumber and yoghurt salad) will already be familiar, but there are many other delights, among them *elma dizmesi*, a dish of apples and meat patties, and *cuvecte yaz turlusu*, a tasty summer stew.

WINE, BRANDY AND BEER

Cypriot wine is plentiful and inexpensive, and it is claimed that it has been made in Cyprus since 2000BC. The main wineries are at Limassol, but, increasingly, smaller producers are developing and some of the villages and monasteries now produce their own wines. It is an important business that is now worth €20 million a year in exports.

Commandaria sweet wine is one of Cyprus's best known wines and it is said that it was drunk during the ancient festivals of Aphrodite. However, its origins can only be definitively traced back to the estate of the Knights Hospitaller at Kolossi, 700 years ago.

The island's brandy can no longer be labelled as such because of an EU directive that insists on a 36 per cent alcohol content. But, with lemons and angostura bitters it still makes fabulous brandy sours. Keo and Carlsberg beers are among those brewed locally.

short break

If you have only a short time to visit Cyprus and would like to take home some unforgettable memories you can do something local and capture the real flavour of the island. The following suggestions will give you a wide range of sights and experiences that won't take very long, won't cost very much and will make your visit very special. If you only have time to choose just one of these, you will have found the true heart of Cyprus.

● **Go to the Roman theatre at Kourion** (➤ 40–41) for classical drama: the atmosphere is electric. Performances are held throughout the year (details from the tourist office).

● **Find a quiet beach,** preferably fringed with bushes or tall grasses, and take a swim long before breakfast.

● **Have a drink in a village coffee shop.** Be prepared to be ignored, but it is much more likely that someone will chance their English and start a conversation.

● **Join a plate-breaking session in a Greek taverna.** This mayhem is not as common as it once was, but enquiries may lead to a venue.

● **Get invited to a village wedding,** witness the chaotic church service and drink and eat all night under the stars.

● **Ski or toboggan on Mount Olympos** (► 155). No chance here for summer visitors – the season is from December or January to the end of March.

● **Have a full alfresco *meze* off the tourist track,** but be prepared to stay awake all night with a distended stomach.

● **Drive to Petra tou Romiou,** or the Rock of Romios – better known as the Rock of Aphrodite (➤ 113) – in the late afternoon and stop on the cliff-top a little to the east. The view is tremendous.

● **Join in a Greek dance.** The impressiveness of the steps is hardly matched by the difficulty. Take a couple of brandy sours first.

● **Walk a forest trail in the Troodos or Pentadaktylos Mountains** until perspiring freely, then sit down and have a picnic.

Planning

Before You Go

WHEN TO GO

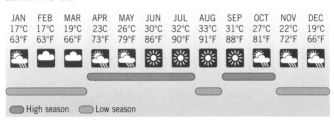

JAN	FEB	MAR	APR	MAY	JUN	JUL	AUG	SEP	OCT	NOV	DEC
17°C	17°C	19°C	23C	26°C	30°C	32°C	33°C	31°C	27°C	22°C	19°C
63°F	63°F	66°F	73°F	79°F	86°F	90°F	91°F	88°F	81°F	72°F	66°F

High season   Low season

Temperatures are the **average daily maximum** for each month on the south coast; there are small variations on the north, west and east coasts. In **Nicosia**, temperatures are approximately an average of 5°C (9°F) higher in summer and 5°C (9°F) lower in the winter; the **Troodos Mountains** are an average 10°C (18°F) cooler than the rest of the country.

The best weather is between March and May and September and November since July and August are very hot and dry.

In winter there are some warm spells, mixed with heavy rain. Snow usually falls in December and January in the Troodos Mountains.

WHAT YOU NEED

● Required
○ Suggested
▲ Not required

Some countries require a passport to remain valid for a minimum period (usually at least six months) beyond the date of entry – check before you travel.

	UK	Germany	USA	Canada	Australia	Ireland	Netherlands	Spain
Passport (or National Identity Card where applicable)	●	●	●	●	●	●	●	●
Visa (regulations can change – check before you travel)	▲	▲	▲	▲	▲	▲	▲	▲
Onward or Return Ticket	▲	▲	▲	▲	▲	▲	▲	▲
Health Inoculations (tetanus and polio)	▲	▲	▲	▲	▲	▲	▲	▲
Health Documentation (► 23, Health Advice)	●	●	●	●	●	●	●	●
Travel Insurance	○	○	○	○	○	○	○	○
Driver's Licence (national)	●	●	●	●	●	●	●	●
Car Insurance Certificate	○	○	n/a	n/a	n/a	○	○	○
Car Registration Document	●	●	n/a	n/a	n/a	●	●	●

ADVANCE PLANNING
WEBSITES
Cyprus Tourist Organization
www.visitcyprus.org.cy
North Cyprus Tourist Information
www.tourism.trnc.net

TOURIST OFFICES AT HOME
In the UK
Cyprus Tourist Office
17 Hanover Street, London
W1S 1YP ☎ 020 7569 8800

Northern Region of Cyprus Tourist
Information Office

29 Bedford Square,
London WC1B 3EG
☎ 020 7631 1930

In the USA
Cyprus Tourism Organization
13 East 40th Street
New York, NY 10016
☎ 212/683 5280

Northern Region of Cyprus Tourist
Information Office
1667 K Street, Suite 690,
Washington DC 20006
☎ 202/887 6198

HEALTH ADVICE
Insurance Tourists get free emergency medical treatment; other services are paid for. For UK nationals benefits are available in the Republic by arrangement with the Department of Health before departure. Medical insurance is advised for all.

Dental services Dental treatment must be paid for by all visitors. Hotels can generally give recommendations for local dentists. Private medical insurance is strongly advised to all tourists to cover costs of dental treatment in Cyprus.

TIME DIFFERENCES

GMT	Cyprus	Spain	USA (NY)	USA (West Coast)	Sydney
12 noon	2PM	1PM	7AM	4AM	10PM

Cyprus is on Eastern European Time from late March to late October (GMT+2).

From late October to late March the time is GMT+3.

WHAT'S ON WHEN
January
New Year's Day (1 Jan)
Epiphany (6 Jan): important Greek Orthodox religious celebration.

March
Greek National Day (25 Mar): parades and celebrations.

April
National Day (1 Apr): anniversary of the EOKA uprising.
National Sovereignty and Turkish Children's Festival (23 Apr).

May
Labour Day (1 May).
May Fair in Pafos (1 May): 10 days of cultural events; exhibitions of flora, basketwork and embroidery.
Anthestiria Flower Festivals (early May): the festivals' origins go back to celebrations honouring the god Dionysos in ancient Greece.
Turkish Youth Festival (19 May).
Cyprus International Fair (late May): the largest trade fair in Cyprus, held in Nicosia and lasting 10 days.

July
Larnaka Festival (throughout Jul): dance and theatre in the fort and the Pattichon amphitheatre.
Peace and Freedom Day (20 Jul): date of Turkish intervention in 1974, public holiday in the North.

August/September
Turkish Communal Resistance Day (1 Aug).
Turkish Victory Day (30 Aug).
Limassol Wine Festival (late Aug–first week in Sep): a 12-day festival, with music and dance.

October
Independence Day (1 Oct).
Greek National Day (28 Oct): also known as Ohi Day. Parades in the South.
Turkish National Day (29 Oct).

November
Proclamation of Turkish Republic of North Cyprus (15 Nov).

NATIONAL HOLIDAYS

JAN	FEB	MAR	APR	MAY	JUN	JUL	AUG	SEP	OCT	NOV	DEC
2		1	1(1)	1(2)	(1)		1		2		3

1 Jan	New Year's Day
6 Jan	Epiphany
25 Mar	Greek National Day
1 Apr	Cyprus National Day
Apr/May	Orthodox Easter
1 May	Labour Day
May/Jun	Pentecost/Kataklysmos (Festival of the Flood)
15 Aug	Assumption of Our Lady
1 Oct	Cyprus Independence Day
28 Oct	Greek National ('Ohi') Day
24–26 Dec	Christmas

Banks, businesses, museums and most shops are closed on these days.

December
Christmas Day (25 Dec).

Moveable feasts
Apokreo Festivities (50 days before Orthodox Easter): two weeks of fun. Limassol has fancy dress balls and children's parades.
Belapais International Music Festival (dates vary).
Green Monday (50 days before Orthodox Easter): a day of laughter, funny disguises and vegetarian picnics in the country.
Procession of Agios Lazaros Icon, Larnaka (eight days before Orthodox Easter Sun): a special Mass service in memory of Agios Lazaros followed by an impressive procession carrying his icon through the town.

Easter: the biggest Greek Orthodox religious feast – on the Sunday, celebrations last all day.
Kataklysmos, Festival of the Flood (50 days after Easter, coinciding with Pentecost): celebrations take place in all the seaside towns and include dancing, folk singing, swimming competitions and boat races.
Agia Napa Festival (late Sep): a weekend of folk music, dance and theatre, combined with agricultural exhibitions.
Seker or Ramazan Bayram: a three-day feast at the end of the Ramadan fast.
Kurban Bayram: four days during which lambs are traditionally sacrificed and shared with the needy.

Getting There

BY AIR
REPUBLIC OF CYPRUS

South Cyprus has two main airports, Larnaka and Pafos. Both are international airports and are served by the national airline Cyprus Airways (☎ 2236 5700; **www.**cyprusairways.com). The two airports and Limassol Harbour are the only recognized points of entry for international visitors.

If you travel to the North and are not a citizen of the European Union, you may be refused entry to the South.

Larnaka Airport is only 5km (3 miles) from the city centre. There is no bus service directly to and from the airport, but taxis are plentiful and inexpensive to Larnaka. If you are travelling to another town, consider taking a bus from Larnaka, otherwise your fare will be high.

Pafos Airport is 10km (6 miles) from the city and buses run six times a day between the city and airport. Taxis to the centre of Pafos are inexpensive, but onward taxi fares rise sharply. As with Larnaka, you might take a taxi to Pafos and continue your journey by bus.

NORTH CYPRUS
International flights arrive at Ercan Airport. There is no public transport from the airport, but taxis run to Nicosia, Keryneia and Famagusta.

BY SEA
Ferries arrive at either Keryneia or Famagusta harbours.

Getting Around

PUBLIC TRANSPORT

REGIONAL BUSES

Republic of Cyprus Intercity buses operate frequently between towns

and various holiday resorts. Almost all villages are connected by local buses to nearest towns but services operate only on weekdays, once a day, leaving in early morning and returning in the afternoon.

North Cyprus Except for the main routes such as Nicosia to Keryneia (Girne), Famagusta (Gazimağusa) or Morfou (Güzelyurt), buses are infrequent, with no timetable.

BOAT TRIPS

Republic of Cyprus One-day boat excursions (usually including lunch) operate from April to October or November. Trips include Limassol Harbour to Lady's Mile Beach; Pafos Harbour to Coral Bay and Agios Georgios; Larnaka Marina along Larnaka, Agia Napa and Protaras; Agia Napa to Paralimni and Protaras; and Lakki along the Akamas coast.

North Cyprus From May to October there are boat trips (including lunch) from Keryneia (Girne) Harbour to the beaches at Acapulco and Alagadi, or to Alsancak, Lapta and Karşiyaka (☎ 815 3708).

URBAN TRANSPORT

Republic of Cyprus Urban and suburban buses operate frequently during the day between 5.30am and 7pm. During summer, in certain tourist areas, buses may operate until midnight. It is a good idea to check routes with your hotel.

North Cyprus There are good bus services within the main towns, with buses running approximately every half hour. Check with your hotel for more detailed information.

TAXIS

In the Republic service taxis, shared with other people (4 to 7 seats), operate between main towns every hour or so. There are also rural taxis that operate in hill resorts and urban taxis in towns.

In the North taxis can only be found at taxi stands.

CAR RENTAL

The many firms on the island include internationally known companies, though there are mainly local ones in the north. Cars, especially out of season, are moderately priced in the Republic and the North.

Drivers must usually be aged between 25 and 75 and have had a licence for more than a year.

CONCESSIONS

Students Cyprus is not really on the backpacker route, but there are youth hostels in Nicosia, Larnaka, Pafos and in the Troodos Mountains. For details contact: The Cyprus Youth Hostel Association, PO Box 24040, CY 1700 Nicosia (☎ 267 0027). The youth card 'Euro<26' secures discounts for ages 13–26 on a wide range of products. Contact the Youth Board of Cyprus, 62 Leoforos Aglantzias, Nicosia (☎ 2240 2600; **www.**Youthboard.org.cy).

Senior citizens Few concessions are made to elderly visitors. Most hotels offer discounts during the low season but these are available to all age groups.

DRIVING

Drive on the left.

Speed limits on motorways and dual carriageways:
100kph (62mph);
min **65kph (40mph)**.
Speed limits on country roads:
80kph (50mph) (North Cyprus: **65kph/40mph**).
Speed limits on urban roads:
50kph (31mph), or as signposted

Seatbelts must be worn in front seats at all times and in rear seats where fitted.

Random breath-testing takes place. Never drive under the influence of alcohol.

Fuel in the north and the Republic of Cyprus is less expensive than much of Europe. Grades sold are super, regular, unleaded and diesel. Fuel stations in the south open 6am–6pm, with automatic credit card/cash vending at other times. In the north they may open until 9 or 10pm.

If you break down in the Republic of Cyprus a 24-hour towing service is provided by the Cyprus Automobile Association in Nicosia (☎ 2231 3131), which is affiliated to the Alliance International de Tourisme (AIT).

If the car is rented follow the instructions given in your documentation.

Being There

TOURIST OFFICES

Republic of Cyprus
- Cyprus Tourism Organization
  PO Box 24535
  CY 1390 Nicosia
  ☎ 2269 1100
  www.visitcyprus.org.cy

- 11 Odos Aristokyprou
  Laïki Geitonia
  Nicosia
  ☎ 2267 4264
- 115A Odos Spyrou Araouzou
  Limassol
  ☎ 2536 2756
- 22 Odos Georgiou A'
  Germasogeia
  ☎ 2532 3211
- Plateia Vasileos Pavlou
  Larnaka
  ☎ 2465 4322
- 3 Odos Gladstonos
  Pafos
  ☎ 2693 2841
- 12 Leoforos Kryou Nerou
  Agia Napa
  ☎ 2372 1796
- Pano Platres
  ☎ 2542 1316
- 2 Odos Vasileos Stasioikou
  Polis
  ☎ 2632 2468

Northern Cyprus
- Nicosia
  ☎ 228 9629
- Keryneia
  ☎ 815 2145
- Famagusta
  ☎ 366 2864

EMBASSIES AND CONSULATES
UK
2286 1100 (RoC)
228 3861 (NC)
Germany
2245 1145 (RoC)
227 5161 (NC)
USA
2239 3939 (RoC)
227 8295 (NC)
Netherlands
2287 3666 (RoC)
Spain
2245 014 0 (RoC)

SUMMER OPENING HOURS (REPUBLIC)

● Shops   ● Banks   ● Museums
● Offices   ● Archaeological sites   ● Pharmacies

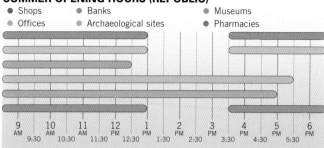

SUMMER OPENING HOURS (NORTH)

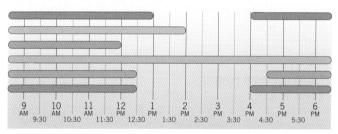

TELEPHONES

In the Republic public telephones are found in town centres. They take 2-, 5-, 10- and 20-cent coins or *telecards* (CY£3, CY£5, CY£10, from banks, post offices, tourist offices or kiosks). Payphones in the North now only accept phone cards, sold in denominations of 100, 200 and 300 units.

INTERNATIONAL DIALLING CODES

From Cyprus to
UK 00 44

USA 00 1
Netherlands 00 31
Spain 00 34
Germany 00 49

EMERGENCY TELEPHONE NUMBERS

Police assistance:
☎ 112 (Republic)
☎ 155 (North)
Fire:
☎ 112 (Republic)
☎ 199 (North)
Ambulance:
☎ 112 (Republic and North)

POSTAL SERVICES
Post offices
There are main post offices in main towns.

Republic: open Mon–Fri 7.30–1.30 (Thu also 3–6). Tel 2230 3219.

North: open Mon–Fri 8–1, 2–5, Sat 8.30–12.30. Tel 228 5982.

ELECTRICITY
The power supply is 240 volts
Type of socket: Square, taking three-square-pin plugs (as UK); in older buildings, round two-pin sockets taking two-round-pin (continental-style) plugs.

CURRENCY AND FOREIGN EXCHANGE
Currency: The currency of the Republic is the Cyprus pound (CY£), divided into 100 cents. Coins are in denominations of 1, 2, 5, 10, 20 and 50 cents; notes CY£1, 5, 10 and 20. The Republic plans to replace CY£ with the euro in 2008.

The currency of North Cyprus is the New Turkish Lira (YTL).

Credit cards and exchange:
Exchange travellers' cheques for Cyprus pounds or New Turkish Lira at banks, bureaux de change and hotels. Many banks have ATMs. Most currencies are accepted at banks, hotel exchanges and shops in both zones.

HEALTH AND SAFETY
Sun advice Cyprus enjoys almost constant sunshine all year. Wear a hat and drink plenty of fluids during the hot months (particularly July and August). A high-protection sunscreen is also recommended.

Drugs Minor ailments can be dealt with at pharmacies (*farmakio* in the south, *eczane* in the north). Pharmacies sell all branded medicines. Some drugs available only on prescription elsewhere are available over the counter.

TIPS/GRATUITIES

Yes ✓   No ✗

Hotels (service included)	✗	
Restaurants (service included)	✗	
Cafés/bars (service included)	✗	
Taxis	✓	10%
Tour guides	✓	CY£1
Porters	✓	CY£1 per bag
Hairdressers	✓	CY£1
Cloakroom attendants	✓	50c
Theatre/cinema usherettes	✗	
Toilets	✗	

Safe water Tap water in hotels, restaurants and public places is generally safe to drink though not very palatable in the north, particularly around Famagusta. Bottled water is widely available and inexpensive.

Personal safety The police are relaxed and helpful and English is widely spoken. In tourist areas in the south, Cyprus Tourism Organization representatives can provide a degree of assistance. However, crime in Cyprus is at a reassuringly low level. Take the usual precautions with regard to handbags and valuables left in cars. Any thefts or offences should be reported to the police, if only for insurance purposes.

● Do not try to cross the Green Line (the dividing line between the two parts) except at official crossing points.

● Keep away from military zones (north or south).

● Do not use roads marked as blocked-off on a map (they may encroach on military zones).

PHOTOGRAPHY
It is forbidden to photograph in both north and south near military camps or other military installations, in museums, and in churches with mural paintings and icons where a flashlight is required.

CLOTHING SIZES

France	UK	Rest of Europe	USA	
46	36	46	36	
48	38	48	38	
50	40	50	40	
52	42	52	42	
54	44	54	44	Suits
56	46	56	46	
41	7	41	8	
42	7.5	42	8.5	
43	8.5	43	9.5	
44	9.5	44	10.5	
45	10.5	45	11.5	Shoes
46	11	46	12	
37	14.5	37	14.5	
38	15	38	15	
39/40	15.5	39/40	15.5	
41	16	41	16	
42	16.5	42	16.5	Shirts
43	17	43	17	
36	8	34	6	
38	10	36	8	
40	12	38	10	
42	14	40	12	
44	16	42	14	Dresses
46	18	44	16	
38	4.5	38	6	
38	5	38	6.5	
39	5.5	39	7	
39	6	39	7.5	
40	6.5	40	8	Shoes
41	7	41	8.5	

Best places to see

1 Akamas Peninsula

A beautiful region of hills, valleys and rocky shores, ideal for rambling, with rich and varied flora and diverse wildlife.

This westernmost extremity is unique in the Greek Cypriot south of the island, not only for its beauty but also for the absence of tourist development. Three areas are now designated protected and no development is permitted. Proposals are still being discussed for the establishment of a national park.

The vegetation is Mediterranean, with large tracts of impenetrable *maquis* interspersed with a thin covering of pine trees and juniper. Autumn flowering cyclamen is everywhere. In places the landscape is impressively stark, with spectacular rock outcrops. On the beaches green and loggerhead turtles still come up to lay their eggs, and occasionally a monk seal may be sighted.

Although there are no metalled roads, the area is becoming popular with trail-bikers and walkers.

Several trails for ramblers have been created, starting at the Baths of Aphrodite, west of Polis. A network of marked paths traverses the hills and information panels outline the types of flora. These are described in a free booklet from the tourist office called *Nature Trails of the Akamas*. The ascent of Mouti tis Sotiras is worth contemplating: it only takes an hour to reach the summit and the view is superb. Needless to say, in summer it is a hot and sticky expedition. An alternative is to take a boat from Lakki for a swim and a picnic in one of the delightful coves, perhaps near Fontana Amoroza (Love's Spring), halfway to Cape Arnaoutis.

➕ 1E ✉ Cyprus's westernmost peninsula 🍴 Baths of Aphrodite Tourist Pavilion Café (££) ❓ Across the road from the café, and at the end of a short path and under trees is the pool called the Baths of Aphrodite

2 Hala Sultan Tekke and Salt Lake

A Muslim holy shrine standing on the shore of a natural landmark, which has very different aspects in winter and summer.

For Turkish Cypriots, the Hala Sultan Tekke's importance is surpassed only by the shrines of

Mecca, Medina and al Aksha (Jerusalem). It was here that the prophet Mohammed's maternal aunt, Umm Haram, was buried in AD649. Apparently, she fell from a donkey and broke her neck while participating in an Arab raid on the island. Three enormous stones were raised to mark her grave and the site became an important place of pilgrimage for Muslims.

The mosque, with its distinctive dome and minaret, was built by the Turks in 1816, though the tomb dates from 1760. Visitors can enter the mosque but must respect the dress code and remove their shoes before entering.

In the summer the surrounding gardens are a relatively cool haven from the heat of the Salt Lake. This is a desert for much of the year, but in winter the lake fills with water and attracts a wide range of migrating birds. The most spectacular of the winter visitors are the flamingos, whose distinctive pink colour makes

an attractive sight, though their numbers have greatly reduced in recent years. In summer the water evaporates, leaving a dusty grey expanse that shimmers in the heat.

The salt was once a significant product in the island's economy, but today it is no longer economically viable to collect. It originates from the nearby sea, seeping up through the porous rocks during the rainy months.

✚ 11C ✉ 3km (2 miles) west of Larnaka on the Kiti road ⊙ Jun–Aug daily 7.30–7.30; Sep–May daily 9–5 🖐 Free, but donation requested 🍴 Taverna (££) at car park 🚌 Bus from Larnaka with drop-off on the main road

3 Kourion

Kourion is the most important archaeological site in the Greek Cypriot south, impressively perched on the cliffs overlooking the sea.

There has been a settlement here since 3300BC, but the first major town was probably built by Mycenaeans around 1400BC. It reached its zenith under the Romans and it is their influence that is most evident from the ruins. It went into decline as it suffered from Arab raiders and the population moved inland. Excavations started in 1873 and have continued ever since.

The Theatre presents the most striking image of the whole site. It seated an audience of 3,500 and was probably built by the early Greeks and then extended by the Romans to allow for gladiatorial combat and for man against animal spectacles.

The Annexe of Eustolios lies just uphill from the Theatre and has an impressive mosaic floor. Further up the hill are the Baths, which also had mosaic floors. The Baths follow the Roman pattern, with a *frigidarium* (cold room), then a *tepidarium* (warm room) and a *caldarium* (hot baths). Mechanisms for heating the water, along with furnaces and tanks, are in evidence.

At the top of the hill west of the Theatre is the Building of the Achilles Mosaic. Constructed around a courtyard, it has a mosaic showing Achilles in disguise revealing his true identity to Odysseus by mistake. There is also a depiction of Ganymede and the Eagle. The house dates from about AD4. A similar house a short

distance down the track has a mosaic showing two gladiators in combat. Also visible are the remains of an aqueduct that brought the settlement's water supply to the Fountain House, traces of which can still be seen. Opposite the Fountain House is the Basilica, which was built in the 5th century. It has fragments of mosaics on the floor and the roof was once supported by 12 columns.

This site covers the main areas of interest, but about 1km (0.5 miles) towards Pafos is the openly accessible Stadium, which once seated 6,000.

🕂 6B ⊠ Off the Limassol–Pafos road 🕓 Apr–May, Sep–Oct daily 8–6; Jun–Aug daily 8–7.30; Nov–Mar daily 8–5. Excavations on the site can close some parts at times Inexpensive 🍴 Café in the nearby tourist pavilion (£) 🚍 From Limassol 🛈 Classical plays or productions of Shakespeare are performed through summer. The tourist office will have the programme

4 Kykkos Monastery

The monastery is the largest and richest religious foundation in Cyprus and is known throughout the Orthodox world.

Kykkos is high and alone in the hills of western Cyprus, but even at 1,318m (4,323ft) above sea level it is overlooked by higher ground. In summer its cloisters and courtyards are cool; in winter, when the mist descends, the temperature drops dramatically. Cypriots make pilgrimages to Kykkos from all over southern Cyprus, and hundreds may

visit in a weekend. These numbers are swollen by sightseers from the holiday centres.

Kykkos was built about 900 years ago to house its icon, the painting of which is attributed to St Luke and was given to a Cypriot monk by Byzantine Emperor Alexius Comnenos for relieving his daughter's sciatica. The present construction is not of great antiquity – fires destroyed earlier buildings and nothing remain from before the 19th century.

In contrast with the spartan conditions of earlier times, today's monks have many modern comforts. Even so, the community has dwindled from hundreds to a handful, and even fewer novices.

The famous icon is called Eleousa. It has been encased in silver for 200 years and anyone attempting to gaze directly on it does so under sufferance of horrible punishment. Photography is not permitted. There is also a small one-room museum with items of interest from the monastery's past, mainly religious regalia and books.

In 1926 a novice called Michaïl Mouskos came to the monastery. He later became Archbishop Makarios III, and president of Cyprus. In those days he would be awake for prayers at 5.30am followed by a frugal breakfast. During the 1950s EOKA campaign the monastery was used by the guerillas for communications and the handling of supplies. Makarios is buried on the hill called Throni, directly above the monastery.

➕ 4D 📧 West of Pedoulas, western Troodos ☎ Museum: 2294 2736 🕐 Monastery: daily early morning to dusk. Museum: Jun–Oct daily 10–6; Nov–May daily 10–4 💰 Free; museum inexpensive 🍴 Café nearby (£)

5 Lara

Lara is the name of a headland on the west coast with sandy bays on each side. This splendid stretch of coast continues up to Koppos Island, opposite which the rough road peters out, and then on to the distant northern cape.

The nearest outpost is Agios Georgios, hardly a village but having a church and harbour and restaurants. It sees the last of the hard surface road, and from now on the track is terrible, best attempted with a 4-wheel-drive vehicle or an off-road motorcycle . And there is quite a lot of it – 8km (5 miles) in all, with one steep area that is a real test of nerve on the cliff edge. Thicket, thorn and mimosa border the road, and only by chance or local knowledge can sandy coves on the rocky shore be found. The beaches of Lara itself are easier to discover, with a sweeping bay to the north and a smaller one to the south.

Lara is now a popular excursion destination and there are regular boat trips from Pafos, calling at

Agios Georgios on the way. Such splendid beaches and scenery would attract visitors in any circumstances, but there is a further incentive – Lara's famous sea turtles.

In an attempt to secure the future of these beleaguered and precious amphibians, a hatchery has been established at Lara. Its opening was accompanied by great publicity and many make the trip in the hope of seeing them; in fact there is no certainty of this – much depends on the cycle of the breeding season. The future of this beautiful and ecologically important coastline has been secured since the government declared that no building development was permitted in the area.

🕂 1D ✉ Western Cyprus, north of Pafos 🍽 Café near the headland (£)

6 Nicosia Walled City

www.nicosia.org.cy

Eleven stout bastions superimposed on a circular wall give the city its distinctive and unique plan. Much has survived across the centuries.

Nicosia's formidable walls, so masterfully constructed by the Venetians, remain substantially intact, though Pafos Gate to the west is battered and Girne (Keryneia) Gate's situation ruined. Famagusta Gate has fared better, although it is now a cultural centre, perhaps something of a comedown for what was the important eastern entrance into the city. A lesser indignity has been

inflicted on the moat (always intended to be dry): this deep and formidable barrier to full-scale attack is now gardens, car parks and football pitches. In the end the great walls did not save Nicosia. The Turks broke through in 1570 after a bloody siege that lasted 70 days.

Today Lidras and Onasagoras streets, in the Greek Cypriot sector, are thriving places, and small shops are continuously busy. A little to the east the reconstructed buildings in the Laïki Geitonia quarter (► 147) are popular. In the Turkish Cypriot part development moves at a somewhat slower pace.

Along the backstreets some areas are conspicuously decrepit. This is not always to be regretted, as low overheads have enabled a Bohemian quarter to grow up around Famagusta Gate, with bars, cafés, a bookshop or two and a small theatre. Close by, and including Odos Ermou, is a renovated neighbourhood. The buildings, mainly houses, remain much as before, but have been refurbished. Small interesting squares, once rough underfoot, are now smoothly paved.

Of course, Nicosia is the city of the Green Line, a barrier of sandbags and barbed wire that can now easily be crossed at several official points, and was erected before the conscripts who now guard it were born.

✚ *Nicosia 1e* ✉ Centre of Nicosia 🍴 Cafés at Laïki Geitonia, Famagusta Gate, Atatürk Meydanı (£)

7 Pafos Mosaics

Roman houses with impressive and well-preserved mosaics depicting colourful scenes from Greek mythology.

The mosaics were discovered in five large 3rd century AD villas that probably belonged to wealthy Roman noblemen (one was presumably the governor's palace). The House of Dionysos was excavated first, after a passing shepherd turned up some fragments of mosaics. The depictions include Ganymede being taken to Olympus by an eagle. The most famous mosaic illustrates the triumph of Dionysos as he heads across the skies in a chariot drawn by leopards. According to the legend, Dionysos was the first person to discover how to make wine, and his followers are depicted enjoying the fruits of his labour.

The House of Aion displays a fine series of late 4th-century mosaics, which were discovered in 1983. The five scenes starting from the top left show Leda and the Swan; the baby Dionysos; then the middle panel portrays a beauty contest being judged by Aion; on the bottom row is the triumphant procession of Dionysos and the punishment of a musician, Marsyas, who had challenged Apollo to a musical contest and lost.

The House of Orpheus contains representations of Amazons, Hercules and the Lion of Nemea, alongside an impressive mosaic of Orpheus.

The main mosaic in the House of Theseus is that of Theseus killing the minotaur, although there are some others featuring Achilles and Neptune. The mosaics here are less well preserved than in other areas of the site. A newer discovery – the House of the Four Seasons – was unearthed in 1992. Mosaics showing the Gods of the Seasons and a variety of hunting scenes were found here. As excavations are continuing, parts of these houses may not be open to the public.

✚ *Pafos 1b* ✉ Within the UNESCO World Heritage Site, a short distance inland from the harbour ☎ 2630 6217
🕐 Jun–Aug daily 8–7.30; Sep–May daily 8–5. Closed 1 Jan, 25 Dec, Greek Orthodox Easter Sun 💷 Moderate (includes Odeion ➤ 124 and Saranda Kolones ➤ 127)
🍴 Cafés at the harbour (££)

8 St Hilarion Castle

This fortified former monastery, besieged and taken by Richard the Lionheart in 1191, has spectacular coastal views.

Richard the Lionheart laid siege to the castle (Agios Ilarion), and after four days the Byzantine ruler Isaac Comnenos surrendered. Today the Turkish military controls the heights around the castle, and it is a significant place to advertise their presence.

This is no compact, easily visited site. There are lower, middle and upper wards, with quite a distance between each and a steep climb to the upper section. The big compensation for the effort – fairly substantial in the summer heat – is the unbelievable view. The north shore is directly below and mainland Turkey is plainly visible in the clear air of the cooler months. East and west a spectacular

line of peaks and ridges runs into the distance.

St Hilarion, it seems, was a recluse who found refuge on these heights, and built a retreat here. A monastery was established on the site in the 11th century, and was later fortified and then extended by the Lusignans. The lower ward housed the garrison and their horses. A tunnel leads on to the middle ward and a small

Byzantine church. Some steps descend to a hall, which may have been a refectory, or banqueting chamber. Adjacent is a belvedere and café. The view over the coast is exceptional.

The path to the upper ward climbs steadily to the mountain top. Even then not everything is accessible, although St John's Tower, in its precipitous location, can be reached by a short detour. The Queen's Window is perhaps the ideal place to stop and rest.

✚ 15K ✉ High in the hills west of Keryneia (Girne)
🕓 Jun–Sep daily 9–4.30; Oct–May daily 9–1, 2–4.45
✋ Moderate 🍴 Café at the gate (£)

9 Salamis

In legend the founder of Salamis, an impressive archaeological site, was the Greek hero Teucer, brother of Ajax, and son of Telamon.

In the 7th century BC Salamis was the first city of Cyprus. It was not until the Roman occupation centuries later that it was succeeded by Pafos in the west. In AD350 the Byzantines changed the city's name to Constantia and restored it as the capital. There was much subsequent rebuilding due to earthquakes, but in the 7th century Arab attacks left the city in ruins.

In high summer a visit is a memorable occasion, although only the most determined will be able to stay the full course in the great heat. However, the Roman Theatre should not be missed, with its restored tiers of seats rising to an impressive height.

A little further north are the vents and hypocausts of the Baths, opening on to the Gymnasium, all built by the Romans. This structure, its rows of marble columns plainly evident, was damaged by earthquakes and remodelled in Byzantine times, only to collapse later. The columns that we see today were re-erected in the 1950s.

South of the Theatre the huge columns of the granite Forum lie across the site. To the east are the few remains of the church of Agios Epifanios, built in the 4th century. This northern section of the site was a cultural centre. The Agora is found in the

central part, near the Voutra, a 7th-century cistern. Close by are the ruins of the Temple of Zeus.

Walk of some 500m (550yds) northeast, towards the sea, and you will come to the Kampanopetra, a large Early Christian basilica, which has been only partially excavated. The Ancient Harbour is about 300m (330yds) southeast, on the shoreline. Alternatively, cross the main road and walk about 200m (220yds) to the western site. Here, at the Royal Necropolis, are several important tombs. These were designed for rich citizens, though there are also tombs for ordinary people nearby, called the Cellarka.

✚ 20J ✉ 10km (6 miles) north of Famagusta (Gazimağusa)
🕒 Jun–Sep daily 9–7; Oct–May daily 9–1, 2–4.45
♿ Moderate 🍴 Café near north entrance (£)

10 Troodos Mountains

Despite their elevation, these are mostly rounded hills with a multitude of charming villages hidden in the pine-clad folds.

The Troodos is an extensive area, running from west of Larnaka to the high ground of Mount Olympos, then falling gradually to the western coast. There are many reasons for taking in the delights of the mountains, and they make a refreshing change from the hot beaches and dusty lowlands. Terraced vineyards shape the lower southern slopes, with Aleppo pine covering the higher ground. Summits may be tree covered or adorned with spiky scrub, relieved occasionally with dried flowers. Northern slopes are different again: dark poplars stand out in the valleys alongside golden oak and rock rose. Summer days are cooler on the high ground and a big attraction in winter is the snow, with skiing on Mount Olympos.

The most impressive of Cyprus's celebrated monasteries are in the Troodos. Chrysorrogiatissa (► 130–131), standing in splendid terrain, is about 45km (28 miles) from Pafos. Kykkos (► 42–43) is

more convenient for Limassol, but still half a day's excursion. In the east is Machairas (➤ 154–155), less splendid, but well worth a visit.

Regrettably few seek out the small Byzantine churches of Panagia tou Araka (➤ 158) and Stavros tou Agiasmati near Lagoudera on the north side of the range. This is understandable, because it is a long drive, but their frescoes are extraordinary.

Walks and trails are now popular in Cyprus, and those above Platres (Kalidonia Falls and around Mount Olympos) are detailed in a booklet produced by the tourist office. In western Cyprus the forest takes over, and Cedar Valley (➤ 78) is renowned for its giant cedars. Fortunately for the peace of this marvellous area few people seem prepared to negotiate the difficult roads.

✚ 4D ✉ Central Cyprus 🍴 Cafés at Troodos resort, Platres, Foini, Kakopetria and other villages (£–££)

Best things to do

Great places to have lunch

Angelos
Simple food in a cliff-top setting overlooking the sea. Popular with locals and visitors alike.

✉ Governor's Beach ☎ 2563 2552

Bunch of Grapes Inn
The building is splendid and unique, the menu a blend of traditional Cypriot dishes and British and French cuisine.

✉ Pissouri village ☎ 2522 1275

Esperia
Excellent seafood in a wonderful position beside the turquoise waters of the harbour.
✉ Harbour, Agia Napa ☎ 2372 1635

Melanda
Specializes in seafood. Sited at the edge of the unspoiled beach.
✉ Avdimou Beach (not the jetty), 30km (18.5 miles) west of Limassol
☎ 2599 1700

Militzis Restaurant
The best of Cyprus's village food.
✉ 42 Odos Piale Paşa, Larnaka ☎ 2465 5867

Petra tou Romiou Restaurant
Fabulous views over the famous Rock of Aphrodite.
✉ Petra tou Romiou ☎ 2699 9005

Set Fish Restaurant
Good harbour position. Wide range of fresh fish every day.
✉ Kordonboyou, Keryneia (Girne) Harbour

Vangelis
Popular with locals. For something traditional try the pigeon or rabbit.
✉ Paralimni on the Deryneia road ☎ 2382 1456

Yiangos & Peter
Fine harbour view; seafood straight off the fishing boats.
✉ Harbour, Latsi ☎ 2632 1411

Yianna Marie
Splendid location, a little way behind the beach.
✉ Fig Tree Bay ☎ 2381 4440

...afts

...d-woven reed baskets are made at
...lofagou and Sotira, near Agia Napa, and
...at Geroskipou.

Ceramics Craft pottery centres include Geroskipou,
Koloni, Omodos and Foini. In the north, visit the
Ceramic Centre at Ortakioi (Ortaköy) (➤ 187).

Embroidery Hand-embroidered *lefkaritika* lace is
made at Lefkara (➤ 112, 118). Fine lace is also
made in North Cyprus.

Glassware Omodos has several glass workshops.

Gourds These are made into plant pots and vases.

Honey Some convents harvest excellent honey.

Icons Made at Agia Varnava Monastery and Panagia
Chrysorrogiatissa (➤ 130–131).

Leather Leather bags, belts and jackets are widely
available.

Silver Lefkara is noted for its silverware (➤ 112,
119).

Weaving Handloom-woven striped, brightly
coloured *lefkonika* cloth is now made at Fyti, near
Pafos (➤ 139).

Woodwork Items are usually made from olive-tree
wood.

Archaeology

Amathous (➤ 104)
These ruins in Limassol, are
spread widely, and possibly
extend into the sea.

Choirokoitia (➤ 110)
Was home to a large
community in the 7th
century BC.

Kition (➤ 88)
The site of the remains of an
ancient city.

Kourion (➤ 40–41)
This is the south's most
important archaeological site.

Odeion (➤ 124)
These Roman ruins in Pafos
have been partially restored.

Pafos (➤ 48–49)
The city has a wealth of
Roman remains, including
some stunning mosaics.

Palaia Pafos (➤ 132–133)
The ruins outide Pafos
includes the Sanctuary of
Aphrodite.

St Hilarion Castle (► 50–51)
This was a fortified monastery
whose ruins are in the
Pentadaktylos (Beşparmak)
Mountains.

St Paul's Pillar (► 125).
The site is still undergoing
excavation,

Salamis (► 52–53)
The leading city of Cyprus in
the 7th century BC, is a large
and impressive site.

Sanctuary of Apollo Ylatis
(► 114).
The temple was a place of
worship for many centuries.

Tombs of the Kings (► 127).
Probably the tombs of noble
families rather than royalty.

Activities

Cycling There are scores of bicycles for rent in all the resorts. Main roads can be very busy at weekends and the tourist office advises cyclists to avoid them at this time.

Diving Explorations of the wonders of the deep are well catered for at diving centres and some hotels around the island.

Golf One has to admire the Cypriots – nothing is too daunting. In brown waterless landscapes they have created greens. This entrepreneurial boldness appears to have paid off with four 18-hole courses now well established (► 140).

Hill walks In summer it is very hot for walking. Nevertheless, interesting trails have been laid out in the Akamas and Troodos.

Horse-back riding There are centres in Nicosia, Limassol and Pafos. Riding trails include countryside areas such as the Troodos Mountains.

Luxuriating and spa treatments Participants welcome the enervating heat and thus stimulated take their ease at poolside, on the terrace or the beach. Increasingly spa treatments are available at hotels.

Parascending Incredibly, people queue for this expensive death-defying adventure. One nervous, critical bound and it is up into the thermals.

WATER SPORTS
Exciting There are more ways of following a motor boat than standing upright on two planks of wood. A multitude of flexible inflatables, including the notorious banana, skim the waves during high speed tows. Some aficionados of the foam prefer the adrenaline boost of jet skis. Windsurfing and surfing are all popular

although some areas are unsuitable for these pursuits. Sailing is catered for, and there are also organized boat trips

Sedate Relaxing pastimes include airbed floating and the ever-popular pedalos.

Swimming Few can resist the warm turquoise sea. You'll see every swimming technique known to man, and some others, performed with great virtuosity.

Places to take the children

Aphrodite Waterpark

Pools, splashes, spiral descents and more.

✉ Geroskipou, off Leoforos Poseidonos ☎ 2691 3638 ⏱ Apr–Oct
daily 10–6

Bird Park

Parrots, hornbills, toucans and eagles and many more species.
Gazelles, giant tortoises and other reptiles plus an aquarium,
cinema and restaurant.

✉ Pegeia on road north out of Coral Bay ☎ 2681 3852 ⏱ Apr–Sep daily
9–8; Oct–Mar daily 9–5

Camel Park

Learn about camels and enjoy a ride, or take a swim in the pool.

✉ Mazatos, 20km (12 miles) southwest of Larnaka ☎ 2499 1243
⏱ Daily 8–6

Donkey Sanctuary

Unwanted donkeys end up here, cared for by two expatriates from the UK. A visitor centre has information and refreshments.

✉ Vouni, 36km (22 miles) northwest of Limassol ☎ 2594 5488
🕐 Daily 10–4

Luna Park

An assembly of wheels, rides, coasters, trampolines and other stomach-churning creations. Plus the notorious Sling Shot and the popular Skycoaster.

✉ Off Leoforos Nissi, adjacent to the Napa Tsokkas Hotel, Agia Napa
🕐 May–Oct daily; no fixed hours

Oasis Luna Park

Big Wheel, scary inclined ride, dodgems and all the fun of the fair.

✉ 107 Leoforos Georgiou A' Potamos Germasogeias, Limassol ☎ 2531 8389
🕐 Times vary, but usually daily

Ocean Aquarium Protaras

Hundreds of species from the seas, plus landscaped grounds.

✉ 19 Leoforos Kavo Gkreko, Protaras, 5km (3 miles) north of the centre
☎ 2374 1111 🕐 Daily 10–8

Snake George's Reptile Park

George tries to improve public understanding of snakes at his reptile park.

✉ 15km (9 miles) north of Pafos on coast road to Agios Georgios, behind EKO petrol station ☎ 9998 7685 🕐 Daily 10–sunset

Wet 'n' Wild Waterpark

Chutes and other ingenious designs flush willing participants through a multitude of coloured tubes.

✉ Off Limassol–Nicosia Highway, Mouttagiaka junction, Limassol ☎ 2531 8500 🕐 Apr–Oct daily 10–6

Beaches

Avdimou Beach

Avdimou Beach (▶ 109) is a good long sandy stretch, though the water becomes deep very quickly. There is a small taverna at each end and it is usually quiet, but at weekends it can be busy with service personnel and their families. It is part of the British Sovereign Base and so has not seen any tourist development.

✉ 3km (2 miles) off main road, opposite turning to Avdimou village

🍴 Taverna on beach (£)

Coral Bay

The small bay comes complete with hotels, shops and restaurants. The sea is a beautiful turquoise but the shoreline is being lost to development. The popular beach has sun beds everywhere and water sports.

✉ 13km (8 miles) north of Pafos 🚌 10, 15 from Pafos lower town

🍴 Cafés on the clifftops (££)

Famagusta Beach

Beautiful and sandy, but near the ruined resort of Varosha.

Governor's Beach

The beach is reached by steps cut out of the steep white cliffs. The astonishingly dark sand is its most distinctive feature and can get painfully hot by the middle of a summer's day. The beach, although narrow, is popular with local people and can be very busy on summer weekends.

✉ Junction 16 Nicosia–Limassol motorway

Karpasia (▶ 79). This ares in North Cyprus has miles of lovely, sandy beaches.

Konnos Bay

North of Cape Gkreko (Greco), this bay has white sands and clear blue sea.

Lara
See pages 44–45.

Nissi Beach
Two kilometres (1 mile) outside Agia Napa. Popular and so likely to be busy in summer (▶ 92).

Pissouri Bay
One of few sandy beaches in the area, this is sure to get busy at times.

Pomos coast
This coast is noted for its quiet sandy beaches (▶ 134).

Timi Beach
Sandy coves and waters that are quiet until the weekends.

Ways to be a local

Adapt to Mediterranean time. Go out late, eat late, don't rush and take everything as it comes.

Wear appropriate dress. Dress respectfully when you visit churches, monasteries and mosques – no shorts or bare shoulders.

Take an afternoon siesta. Stay out of the hot summer sun. Retreat into the shade to sleep or spin out a relaxed lunch.

Browse the bazaars. Also visit the weekly fruit and vegetable markets for unrivalled value and local colour.

Buy hand-made Lefkara lace. Take a look at traditional lace and other embroidery work. Traditionally, a Cypriot bride had to have 100 sheets and pillowcases in her dowry – but you can start a collection with just one beautiful piece.

Order a strong coffee. Visit a traditional village coffee shop, sit back and watch the menfolk gossip and play cards and backgammon.

Linger over an alfresco dinner. Why not sample *meze* dishes? With a range of up to 30 items to choose from, you can try something different every night.

Travel by bus and service taxis. These offer a cheap and friendly alternative to rented cars and ordinary taxis.

Locals don't get drunk in public. You shouldn't either as they will be offended if you do.

Enjoy exotic butterflies. Cyprus has some lovely species, such as the Cleopatra and the two-tailed pasha.

a walk in Limassol (Lemesos)

The walk starts on the seafront by the car parks and sculpture park. Follow the promenade southwest to reach a small roundabout which marks the old harbour, complete with fishing boats. There is a small reptile house on one corner with local and foreign species.

Proceed inland to the 14th-century castle and Cyprus Medieval Museum (▶ 106–107). Turn right along Odos Genthliou Mitella and pass the Al-Kebir mosque, which is still in use.

This was once the Turkish part of the town and many of the older houses are of a typical Turkish design. The municipal fruit and vegetable market lies just east of the mosque.

Continue generally northeast until the road leads into Odos Agiou Andreou, the main shopping street.

There are many narrow alleyways in this area and they are interesting to explore, though walkers should not worry about getting lost as they will eventually emerge on to the wider thoroughfare. Odos Agiou Andreou has a wide range of shops, with goods ranging from the usual souvenirs to leather goods and jewellery.

After about 1km (0.5 miles) Agia Trias Church can be visited a short way up Odos Agias Trias, just before Odos Zinonos Kitieos. Returning to the main road the Folk Art Museum is found a little way on to the left. One kilometre (0.5 miles) further along Odos Agiou Andreou, at the north side of the Municipal Gardens, turn right on Odos Kanningkos to reach the District Archaeological Museum (▶ 107), 200m (210yds) to the left. The walk ends in the Municipal Gardens, which offer peace after the busy city streets.

Distance: 2.5km (1.5 miles)
Time: 1–3.5 hours
Start point Seafront car park
End point Municipal Gardens
Lunch Many cafés opposite the castle (£) ✉ Odos Eirinis

Best views

Belapais Abbey
From its setting in the mountains, you see citrus and almond groves below (➤ 172).

Cape Gkreko (Greco)
The cape is fenced off, but there are views across the coastline from nearby cliffs.

Cape Kormakitis
On a clear day, you can see the Taurus Mountains in Turkey from here.

Chrysorrogiatissa Monastery (➤ 130–131).
Views across the foothills of the Troodos Mountains.

Mount Olympos
Tremendous views across Cyprus (➤ 155).

Pomos Point
Stretch of coastline that has superb views (➤ 79).

St Hilarion Castle
Excellent views reward a stiff climb to castle remains (➤ 50–51).

Stavrovouni
The monastery (➤ 95) has wonderful views across the Larnaka area.

Throni Hill
Views from the hill near Archbishop Makarios' tomb.

Tombs of the Kings
Sweeping views across the sea (➤ 127).

Places to stay

Columbia (££)

The hotel is somewhat isolated from Pissouri village, although this is a benefit during the peak visitor season in mid-summer. There are sea views from all the rooms. Sports facilities include a swimming pool and tennis courts. A shuttle bus runs into the town.

✉ Pissouri Bay ☎ 2522 1201; www.columbia-hotels.com

Dome (££)

See page 97.

Golden Bay (££–£££)

One of Cyprus's best resort hotels. Good standard of comfort in the 193 rooms, and water sports on the beach. There are also two pools, one indoor and one outside.

✉ Larnaka–Dekeleia road ☎ 2464 5444; www.lordos.com.cy

Hilton Cyprus (£££)

Nicosia's most expensive hotel, a prestigious establishment on elevated ground on the south side of the city, complete with large swimming pool and extensive facilities.

✉ Leoforos Archiepiskopou Makariou III, Nicosia ☎ 2237 7777; www.hilton.com

Konnos Bay (££)

This complex has 20 apartments, set around a swimming pool, as well as hotel accommodation. Families will welcome the gently shelving sandy beach.

✉ Kavo Gkreko ☎ 2383 1326

Linos Inn (££)

The inn occupies several restored old houses in the conservation area. Character exudes from wooden beams, four-poster beds and antiques. However, the rooms have modern facilities –

whirlpool baths, satellite television and heating in winter. The
restaurant is to be recommended.

✉ Odos Palaias 34, Kakopetria ☎ 2292 3161; www.linos-inn.com.cy

Le Meridien Limassol Spa & Resort (£££)

Excellent in every respect, including sumptuous well-planned
rooms, splendid indoor and outdoor pools and lawns that sweep
down to the shore. Residents-only operation allows privacy and
exclusive use of all facilities.

✉ Leoforos Amathous ☎ 2586 2000; www.lemeridien-cyprus.com

Palm Beach (£££)

See page 179.

Park Mansion (£–££)

A restored 18th-century mansion in Upper Pafos. Cool tiled floors
in the rooms are welcome in summer. The restaurant is excellent.

✉ Odos Pavlou Mela 16, Ktima, Pafos ☎ 2624 5645

Salamis Bay Conti Resort (£££)

See page 180.

Off the beaten track

Akamas's Gorges

A few companies, including Exalt Travel of Pafos (☎ 2694 3803), run tours through the gorges, the Avakas being the favourite. It is quite an adventure, negotiating the boulder-strewn river bed with sheer cliffs on either side. If the weather is, or is likely to be bad, avoid the gorges – flash floods here can be dangerous.

Avdimou Coast

Drive to Avdimou Beach (➤ 109), about 30km (18.5 miles) west of Limassol, but take the gravel track to Melanda Taverna, not the road to Avdimou Jetty to the east. The beach is often deserted but the cliff-top path running west is a delight, with wonderful views over the coastal strip, and leads to the high cliiffs above Pissouri beach. There is however no need to go more than 200m (218 yards) to find solitude. Occasionally Royal Air Force fighter jets perform manoeuvres offshore, not very peaceful, but spectacular.

Cedar Valley

This is best reached from Pafos, (Pano) Panagía (➤ 133) being the last outpost before setting out on the unmetalled track into the western forest. The valley is 12km (7.5 miles) away: a good map is needed and a jeep is the best vehicle. At 400m (1,312ft) above sea

level, under the canopy of trees, the air is cool. The cedars are magnificent and the stillness is only likely to be disturbed by a moufflon (wild sheep), or the trickle of water from a spring.

Famagusta Bay

The stretch of coast starting about 9km (6.5 miles) north of
Protaras has some fine cliff-top walks. Access is not entirely
obvious. Once on the low escarpments all is straightforward, a
bonus being the view of the crumbling suburbs of Famagusta
(Gazimağusa; ➤ 166) – take binoculars.

Karpasia (Karpaz) Peninsula

Much of northern Cyprus is quiet, but the Karpasia peninsula is
even quieter, with only the locals going about their business. Take
a map and simply set off on a journey of exploration stopping at
any beach, ancient site or village that attracts your attention.

Mandria Shore

Turn into Mandria village, east of the road to Pafos airport. Follow
the beach signs to Pasa church and after 500m (545yds) you will
reach a T-junction. Go left for another 500m (545yds) and turn right
to reach the shore after 1km (0.5 miles), with its shingle beach.

Petounda Point

Take the road west of Kiti village towards Petounda Point for about
6km (3.5 miles). Turn left at the sign for Panagia Petounda Church
and after about 1.5km (1 mile) you will see the church on the right,
but keep left to reach the shore. There are two houses, but a short
walk to the west brings isolation.

Pomos Point to Kato Pyrgos

This section of coast, northeast of Polis in the west, sees fewer
visitors than most others in southern Cyprus. Several stretches of
dark sand line the various bays and coves. The further east you go
the quieter it is. Here the Troodos Mountains descend dramatically
to the sea. In the event of a sudden influx of tourist buses there is
the opportunity to retreat quickly into the quiet hills and gaze down
on the coast from on high.

Interesting diversions

View the forbidden city of Famagusta (Gazimağusa) through binoculars from the roof of an enterprising Greek Cypriot's house in Deryneia (➤ 91). There is a small charge.

Walk the boards at Harmony Park, Limassol (Lemesos). A 6km (3.5-mile) shore walk has been built westwards from San Raphael Marina. All of it runs close to the water's edge but the central timber section is especially cool and pleasant.

Walk the Green Line in the walled city of Nicosia. The Green Line has lost some of its sting since the partial opening of the border in 2003, but it still exists and still exerts a peculiar fascination.

Visit the Keo distillery and winery in Limassol at 1 Leoforos Fragklinou Rousvelt ☎ 2585 3100.

Walk a gorge in the Akamas. Exalt Travel in Pafos (☎ 2694 3803), will arrange a guided excursion.

Hire a pedalo on Agia Napa beach and paddle through the unusual weathered rock formations at the east end of the bay.

Take a 2- or 3-day boat trip from Limassol to Israel and Egypt. Local travel agents will provide all details. Try Louis Cruise Lines in Limassol (☎ 2557 0000).

Visit the Grivas Museum on the beach near Chlorakas and see the wooden ship, *Agios Georgios*, used for gun running during the EOKA campaign.

See the sunrise over the Pentadaktylos Mountains from the Mesaoria (central plain). Spectacular effects reward a spectacularly early start.

Watch the vultures on Mount Pentadaktylos (Beşparmak, east of Keryneia/Girne). Drive to the pass, but go at the weekend when the nearby quarry is closed.

Exploring

In the south there are 340km (211 miles) of coast to explore, along with the fascinating Troodos Mountains and the towns of Larnaka (Larnaca), Limassol (Lemesos), Pafos (Paphos) and Nicosia (Lefkosia). Visitors in the north have to be content with long unspoiled shores, including the fabled Karpasia peninsula and the magnificent Pentadaktylos (Beşparmak) Mountains. The extensive Mesaoria plain is there for good measure.

The Cypriots have long had a reputation for being friendly and welcoming. This extra special reception is no longer common in the busy resorts and perhaps will soon be lost for ever, but it can still catch you unawares in a mountain village or the old quarter of Nicosia.

Larnaka and the Southeast

This part of Cyprus was once the agricultural heartland and it still provides the bulk of the Cypriot potato crop, which thrives in the distinctive red soil. However, in the last 20 years the agricultural industry has been supplanted by tourism, focused on two, previously quiet, resorts – Agia Napa and Protaras. The growth of these areas has been dramatic and Agia Napa today has around 20,000 tourist beds.

Beaches are the main attraction of this region, and the coastline offers a good range of places worth stopping at, although crowds tend to descend on summer weekends. The other attractions of the area are more low key: some traditional villages, Larnaka (Larnaca), the largest town, and a glimpse of the formerly 'forbidden city' of Famagusta (Gazimağusa).

Larnaka (Larnaca)

Larnaka is a significant tourist and commercial centre and is a
convenient base for exploring the island, though its own places of
interest are fairly limited. The modern city is built on the remains
of ancient Kition, which was, according to the legend, established
by one of Noah's grandsons in the 13th century BC. Out of this
settlement Larnaka became an important trading centre, from
where the island's main export of copper was shipped, and it has
long had a large foreign population.

The town can be very busy at rush hour and the narrow streets
and one-way system do not help the foreign driver. Visitors should
try to park quickly and explore on foot. The pedestrianized seafront
is lined with cafés and at the northern end of the promenade is a
large marina with berths for 450 yachts. Larnaka is the main
yachting centre of the island and the port facilities here attract
boats from all over the eastern Mediterranean. There is a very
popular beach, but it is man-made and is certainly not among the
best on Cyprus. The seafront road provides amenities for tourists
with an abundance of cafés, restaurants and ice-cream sellers.

Larnaka has a long history, but much of the evidence has been
covered by the modern city. However the enthusiastic will be able
to track down archaeological remains
and a few historic churches.

 11D

AGIOS LAZAROS CHURCH

Legend states that St Lazarus, having
been raised from the dead by Christ,
came to Larnaka to live out the rest of
his days and when he finally died he
was buried here. His remains,
however, were stolen and only his
empty tomb is visible in the south
apse. The church was built in the
9th century and restored in the

17th century, including the decoration of its extremely ornate interior. There is a small museum inside the building.

➕ *Larnaka 3d* ✉ Odos Agiou Lazarou ☎ Museum 2465 2498 ⏰ Apr–Aug daily 8–12.30, 3.30–6.30; Sep–Mar daily 8–12.30, 2.30–5. Museum: closed Sun and Wed and Sat pm ✋ Museum: inexpensive

ARCHAEOLOGICAL MUSEUM

This museum has a good collection of exhibits – some date back to 3000BC – from Kition (➤ 88) and Choirokoitia (➤ 110). The first room contains statues and terracotta figurines. The pottery collection occupies the second room, along with some Mycenaean vases. Other rooms contain neolithic items, including a reconstruction of a tomb, and finally some Roman glassware. The garden fragments of statues and a mosaic pavement.

➕ *Larnaka 3e* ✉ Odos Kalograion ☎ 2463 0169 ⏰ Mon–Wed, Fri 9–2.30, Thu 9–2.30, 3–5. Closed 1 Jan, afternoons Jul–Aug, 25 Dec ✋ Inexpensive
🍴 Cafés nearby (£)

KITION

The remains of the ancient city can be found at a number of sites. The most visible ruins are on Leontiou Machaira near the Archaeological Museum. The ditches and walls date from the 12th and 13th centuries BC, when they enclosed the city. It is also possible to make out the traces of a Phoenician temple, and the sharp eyed may detect images of ships carved into the south wall.

✚ *Larnaka 3e* ✉ Odos Leontiou Machaira 🕓 Mon–Wed, Fri 9–2.30, Thu 9–2.30, 3–5. Closed afternoons Jul–Aug, 1 Jan and 25 Dec 💷 Inexpensive

PIERIDES MUSEUM

This museum was founded in 1974 to house the private collection of antiquities of Demetrios Pierides, covering the neolithic period to the Middle Ages. The collection, of 3,600 exhibits, is displayed

in the Pierides family's fine 19th-century house, and contains early pottery decorated with various designs, items from the site at Marion, mainly jugs and vases, and one of the most important collections of Roman glassware and jewellery in Europe. The main hall has some early maps of Cyprus and traditional folk artefacts.

✦ *Larnaka 3d* ✉ Odos Zinonos Kitieos ☎ 2481 7868 🕙 Mon–Thu 9–4, Fri, Sat 9–1. Closed 1 Jan, 25 Dec, Greek Orthodox Easter Sun 💷 Moderate
🍴 Cafés nearby (£)

TURKISH FORT AND MEDIEVAL MUSEUM

The fort was built in 1625 by the Turks to defend the city against

raiders but was soon adapted for use as a prison. It now contains a small medieval museum, featuring mainly suits of armour. There are also some artefacts from Kition (► opposite) and other excavations in the area. In summer

theatrical performances sometimes take place in the courtyard.

✦ *Larnaka 3d* ✉ Larnaka seafront, south end of Odos Ankara ☎ 2430 4576
🕙 Jul–Aug Mon–Fri 9–7.30; Sep–May Mon–Fri 9–5. Closed 1 Jan, 25 Dec
💷 Inexpensive 🍴 Cafés nearby (££)

What to See in the Southeast

AGIA NAPA

This major resort stretching along the coast has a reputation for clubs and bars. The town centre retains some appeal with its monastery and adjoining square, and the beaches are excellent, but crowded in summer.

Agia Napa Monastery and its gardens are a welcome haven. Its church was built in the 16th century over a cave where an icon of the Virgin Mary was supposedly found. Within a century the monastery had grown rich, owning much land. It was abandoned in the 18th century but later restored under British rule.

The exhibits at the **Marine Life Museum** include a large number of fossils and shells from Cyprus's waters. A reconstruction of the seabed displays turtles and sharks. One section features marine fauna of the late Cretaceous period and even shows dinosaurs.

Among the sculptures, engravings, vases and ceramics at the **Museum of the Sea** is a full-size replica of the ancient ship

Kyrenia 2 and a papyrus vessel of 9200BC. The museum also has art exhibits and hosts concerts.

✚ 21G

Monastery
✉ Centre of Agia Napa village ⏰ Daily ✋ Free 🍴 Many cafés nearby (££)

Marine Life Museum
✉ 25 Odos Agias Mavris
☎ 2372 3409
⏰ Mon–Wed, Fri–Sat 9–2; Tue 9–2, 3–6 ✋ Moderate
🍴 Many cafés nearby (££)

Museum of the Sea
✉ Town Square opposite the monastery ⏰ Tue–Wed, Fri–Sat 9–2; Tue 9–2, 3–6 ✋ Moderate 🍴 Café in complex

DERYNEIA
This village gives an insight into recent Cypriot history. It is the nearest settlement to Famagusta and one villager has set up a viewing point where tourists, for a small fee, can climb up to the roof of his house and look through a telescope across to the closed Famagusta suburb of Varosha.

✚ 20H ✉ 11km (7 miles) north of Agia Napa 🍴 Café in village (£), restaurant on road to Paralimni (££) 🚌 From Protaras, in summer every hour 8–3, Sun last bus 1.30

HALA SULTAN TEKKE AND SALT LAKE
See page 38–39.

NISSI BEACH

Nissi Beach is where tourist development in this area started. It is

a pleasant sandy beach, though it can be very crowded in summer, with a rocky island just offshore. The presence of a sand bar makes it possible to wade to the island, an adventure that appeals especially to children. Those going to the island should, however, bear in mind that it is made up of rough and spiky rocks and suitable footwear is necessary.

➕ 21G ✉ 2km (1 mile) west of Agia Napa 🍴 Several cafés (£)

PANAGIA ANGELOKTISTI CHURCH (KITI CHURCH)

Panagia Angeloktisti, which means 'built by angels', was constructed in the 11th century on the remains of a 5th-century church. It has many ornate icons but its main attraction is a mosaic that depicts angels attending the Virgin Mary as she holds Christ; it is a very intricate composition, of a style not found elsewhere in Cyprus. The mosaic will be lit up for visitors on request.

➕ 11C ✉ Edge of the village on road to Mazotos ☎ 2442 4646 🕓 Daily 8–12, 2–4. If locked ask for the key at the nearby café 👋 Donation requested 🍴 Café nearby (£) 🚌 From Larnaka

POTAMOS TOU LIOPETRI

This pleasant creek serves as a small fishing harbour. At the shoreline there is a taverna and a long, if slightly rocky, beach with the church of Agios Georgios at its western end. Early in the morning, when the fishermen are returning with their catch, it is a lovely place. The beach is usually quiet and provides an opportunity for calm, safe swimming.

➕ 20G ✉ 14km (8.5 miles) west of Agia Napa 🍴 Taverna on beach (££)

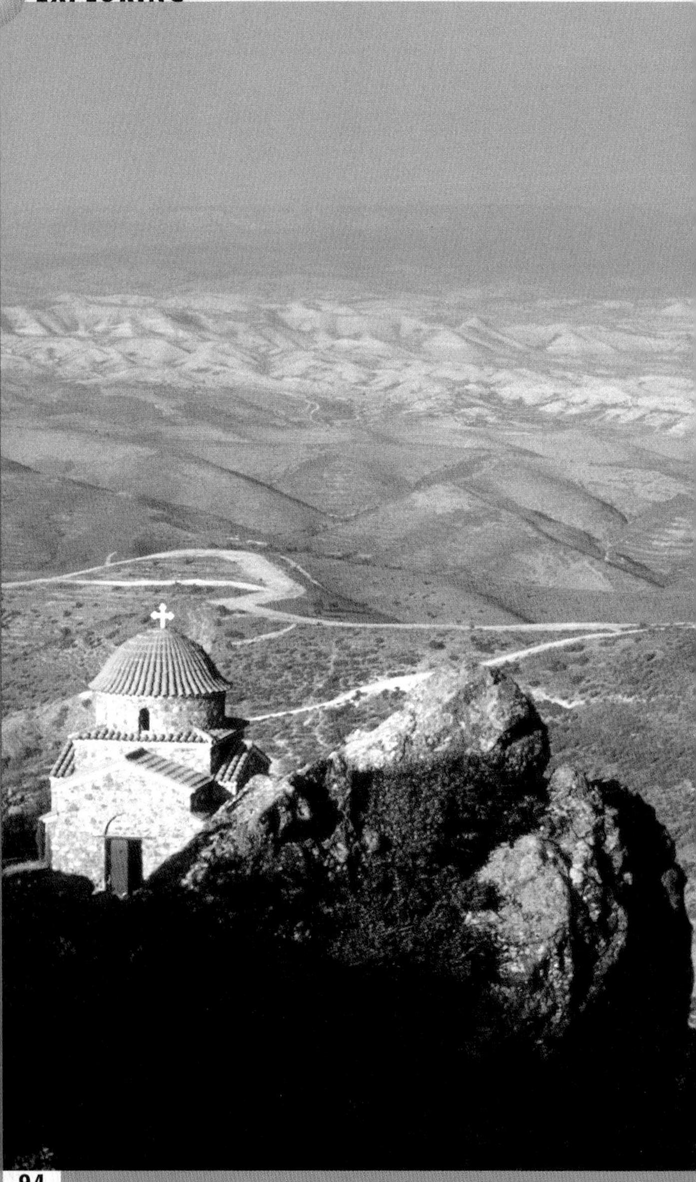

PROTARAS

Protaras, also known as Fig Tree Bay
because of a fig tree that was once its
only landmark, is a fully fledged resort full
of hotels, restaurants and dance clubs.
The beach is sandy and there are good
water sports facilities. The offshore rocky
islet offers the chance of some small
degree of seclusion although you have to
be a fairly strong swimmer to reach it.

✚ 21H ✉ 8km (5 miles) north of Cape Gkreko
(Greco) on east coast 🍴 Numerous cafés and
restaurants (£–££) 🚌 From Agia Napa in
summer: every hour 9–5, Sun 10–5

STAVROVOUNI MONASTERY

The monastery of Stavrovouni, at an
altitude of 690m (2,263ft), has spectacular
views from the top of the hill. There has
been a religious community here since
AD327 when St Helena brought a
fragment of the True Cross from
Jerusalem. It is claimed that the piece is
still in the monastery, covered by a silver
casing. The original buildings were
destroyed by Arab and Turkish raiders and
those visible today date mainly from the
17th century. They are still occupied by a
devout community of monks and women
are not allowed inside.

✚ 10C ✉ 40km (25 miles) west of Larnaka
🕐 Men only. Apr–Aug daily 8–12, 3–6;
Sep–Mar daily 8–12, 2–5 ✋ Free

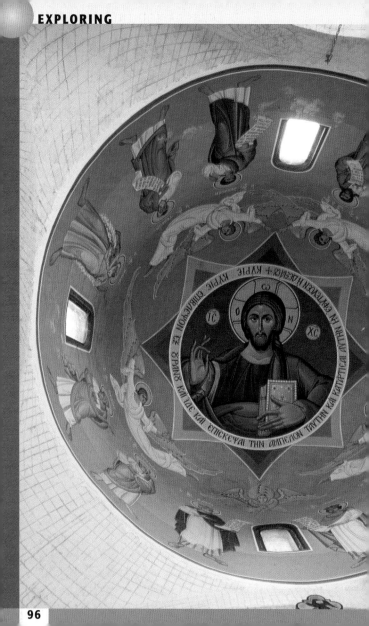

HOTELS

AGIA NAPA

Aeneas (£££)
The hotel is close to the beach of Nissi Bay. Low-rise buildings surround a large swimming lagoon set among pleasant gardens.
✉ Leoforos Nissi ☎ 2372 4000; www.aeneas.com.cy

Dome (££)
A large four-star hotel overlooking two beaches. Lush gardens surround a good-size swimming pool.
✉ Makronisos ☎ 2372 1006; www.domehotel.com.cy

Faros (£)
Exceedingly good location for the town and harbour and away from the busiest roads. The rooms are good and the central pool area excellent.
✉ Leoforos Archiepiskopou Makariou III ☎ 2372 3838;
www.faroshotel.com.cy

Grecian Bay (££)
Directly overlooking the sands of the bay, this hotel has a wide choice of facilities including poolside dining and cool mimosa gardens.
✉ 32 Leoforos Kryou ☎ 2384 2000; www.grecian.com.cy

Nissi Beach (££)
The first hotel to be built at this wonderful little bay, it stands at the edge of the golden sands. The facilities are extensive.
✉ Leoforos Nissi ☎ 2372 1021; www.nissi-beach.com

Olympic Lagoon Resort (££)
The hotel is west of the town and built around a lagoon of rocky waterfalls and whirlpools. It is 100m (110yds) to the beach.
✉ Xylophagou–Agía Napa road 3km (2 miles) to resort centre
☎ 2372 2500; www.kanikahotels.com

LARNAKA (LARNACA)
Cactus (£)
A family-run hotel that remains popular with visitors. Simple but smart rooms and friendly staff. The hotel has a small pool.
✉ 6–8 Odos Saixpird ☎ 2462 7400; www.cactus.com.cy

Lordos Beach (££)
On the shores of Larnaka Bay, north of town, this resort hotel with pool and its own small beach has sea-facing balconies.
✉ Dhekelia Road ☎ 2464 7444; www.lordos.com.cy

Louis Princess Beach (££)
The complex has an international feel. Its 138 rooms are arranged around a good sized pool and terraces. Next to the beach.
✉ Dhekelia Road, 6km (3.5 miles) from the town ☎ 2464 5500; www.louishotels.com

Sun Hall (£)
Close to the town beach and well placed for exploring old Larnaka. The outdoor swimming pool is heated in the chillier months.
✉ Leoforos Athinon ☎ 2465 3341

PROTARAS
Pallini (£)
These hotel apartments are right on splendid Fig Tree Bay and although away from the main road near the town.
✉ Fig Tree Bay ☎ 2283 1900

Pernera Beach (££)
A good retreat by a small beach, midway between Protaras and Paralimni (about 3 km/2 miles to each).
✉ Pernera ☎ 2383 1011; www.pernera.com.cy

RESTAURANTS

AGIA NAPA
Arcadia (££)
This family-run taverna on a side street uphill from the centre of

Agia Napa serves good *meze*, steaks and grills.
✉ 1 Odos Belogianni ☎ 2372 1479 ⏰ Daily

Hokkaido (££)
Japanese food of a high standard. Well designed interior.
✉ 35 Odos Agias Mavris ☎ 2372 1505 ⏰ Daily

Limelight Taverna (££)
One of a handful of local tavernas that have maintained a
reputation for Greek dishes and grills.
✉ Odos Liperti ☎ 2372 1650 ⏰ Daily

Vassos (££)
Popular with locals and visitors alike, and rightly so, thanks to its
excellent seafood. Right at the harbour
✉ Agia Napa Harbour ☎ 2372 1884 ⏰ Daily

LARNAKA (LARNACA)
Alexander (£)
A good budget option offering decent Cypriot food and friendly
service.
✉ 102 Leoforos Athinon ☎ 2465 5544 ⏰ Daily

Archontiko (££)
Cypriot dishes in an attractive restaurant beside the seafront.
✉ 24 Leoforos Athinon ☎ 2465 5905 ⏰ Daily

Dionyssos Fish Tavern (££)
On the seafront, this restaurant has survived the test of time with
its excellent seafood.
✉ 7B Odos Ankara ☎ 2465 3658 ⏰ Daily

Kantara (££)
The restaurant is in new and impressive premises. The well
prepared and nicely presented food is always good.
✉ 2 Odos Salaminas, Dhekelia Road, opposite Karpasiana Hotel ☎ 2464
7000 ⏰ Daily

1900 Art Cafe (££)

Sophisticated local cuisine, home baked sweets and dried herbs in a restored old house with antique furnishings and modern art.

✉ 6 Odos Stasinou ☎ 2465 3027 🕒 Wed–Mon 6–12

Paparazzi (££)

The excellent food is complemented by the pleasant atmosphere.

✉ 35 Leoforos Athinon ☎ 2465 3988 🕒 Daily

Pyla Tavern (££)

Simple fish taverna that is popular with Cyriot families.

✉ Frenaritis complex, Larnaka–Dhekelia road ☎ 2464 5990 🕒 Daily

PROTARAS

Constantia (££)

Family restaurant in a good setting along the road from Cape Gkreko (Greco). The extensive menu suits all tastes.

✉ Konnos Bay ☎ 2383 1946 🕒 Daily in summer

Spartiatis (££)

A bright, modern taverna that hasn't lost its touch with traditional Cypriot fare, Spartiatis has a fine sea view and complements it with seafood fresh from the nearby harbour.

✉ Konnos Beach ☎ 2383 1386 🕒 Daily

Yianna Marie (££)

Serves breakfast, lunch and dinner and all are rather good. The location is marvellous, set just back from the beach.

✉ Fig Tree Bay, north end ☎ 2381 4440 🕒 Daily

SOTIRA

To Ploumin (££)

It would be hard to find more authentic country-style food than at this rambling 1930s farmhouse decked out with old family photographs, rusty farming implements and antiques. You can dine in the courtyard in summer.

✉ 3 Odos Oktovriou 28 ☎ 2373 0444 🕒 Daily

SHOPPING

JEWELLERY SHOPS

Infinity
Well-designed glass and silver items. Lacework, too.
✉ In front of Trizas Hotel, Fig Tree Bay, Protaras ☎ 2383 1989

Sophia Gold and Diamond
A touch of elegance with reasonable prices.
✉ 73 Odos Zinonos Kitieos, Larnaka ☎ 2465 8106

SOUVENIR, HANDICRAFTS AND LEATHER
Laïki Geitonia (traditional quarter) at the south end of Odos
Zinonos Kitieos has a few shops of interest, although type and
ownership change often. About 750m (800yds) to the south on
Odos Boz Kourt and Odos Ak Nteniz are some pottery shops.

Cyprus Handicraft Service
This Ministry of Commerce and Industry shop has traditional
Cypriot crafts: Lefkara lace, silverware, woven cotton, baskets etc.
✉ 6 Odos Kosma Lysioti, Larnaka ☎ 2430 4327

Emira Pottery
Handmade pots of all types and sizes.
✉ 13 Odos Mehmet Ali, Larnaka ☎ 2462 3952

Fotoni's Pottery
✉ 28 Boz Kourt, Larnaka ☎ 2465 0304

Kornos village
Terracotta pottery is produced here as it was 2,000 years ago.

Liopetri and Xylofagou villages
Traditional basket-making.

Mary's Tourist Shop
Leather goods, Lefkara lace and handmade souvenirs.
✉ 26 Odos Zinonos Kitieos, Larnaka ☎ 2465 4393

STORES AND ARCADES
Debenhams
A store selling everything, including records, jewellery and lingerie. It also has a food hall and a bookshop.
✉ Odos Ypsipylis ☎ 2463 1111

Forum
This modest emporium features well-designed quality goods.
✉ 102 Odos Zinonos Kitieos, Larnaka ☎ 2465 9200

ENTERTAINMENT AND SPORT

THEATRE AND CULTURAL EVENTS
Agia Napa Festival (September)
In front of the monastery, with folk music and dancing.
☎ 2381 6300

Larnaka Festival (July)
Dance, theatre and music at the fort and the Patticheion Municipal Theatre.
☎ Information 2465 7745

HORSE-BACK RIDING
Moonshine Ranch
✉ Kavo Gkreko Road, opposite Grecian Bay Hotel, Agia Napa
☎ 9960 5042

SAILING
Larnaka Marina
Facilities for visiting yachts.
☎ 2465 3110

TEN-PIN BOWLING
Virtuality Bowling Center
✉ 24 Odos Eleftherias, Agia Napa ☎ 2372 3290 🕓 Daily 11am–midnight

Limassol and the Southwest

**This region has
something for all tastes
and all interests: an
attractive coastline, a
medieval castle, spectacular views,
archaeological sites and, for the mythologically or
romantically inclined, the birthplace of Aphrodite.**

Anyone interested in history will find plenty to occupy them. The
9,000-year-old site at Choirokoitia is the oldest settlement on the
island, while Kourion and its restored amphitheatre has relics from
the Mycenaean, Persian and Roman periods. There are links with
mythology too – a temple to Apollo – and, at Petra tou Romiou,
the place where Aphrodite is said to have emerged from the
foaming sea. A newer tradition, only 500 years old, is found in the
lacemaking village of Lefkara, and beyond Limassol (Lemesos) are
the vital ingredients for any Cypriot holiday, some good beaches.

Limassol (Lemesos)

Limassol's main claim to fame is that England's Richard the Lionheart was shipwrecked here and married his fiancée Berengaria in the town. The Knights Hospitaller developed Limassol as a trading post based on export of the Commandaria wine, which they made from the vineyards surrounding Kolossi. However, it was only in the 19th century that its major asset, the deep-water port, began to be appreciated and the town became a significant commercial centre.

In recent years Limassol has seen massive tourist development along the wide and noisy approach road on a stretch of coast without good beaches. It is a modern town but it does not lack atmosphere and has good shopping, nightlife and restaurants. The carnival in spring and the wine festival in early September are particularly lively times to visit the town.

The sights of Limassol are easily explored on foot, indeed cars encounter traffic problems and a fiendish one-way system. The main historical sight is the castle and medieval museum. There are also a couple of mosques – reminders of Limassol's Turkish quarter. The main shopping area is around Odos Agiou Andreou.

✚ 7B

AMATHOUS

These archaeological remains are spread widely and include a rock-cut tomb in the grounds of the Amathus Beach Hotel. The most easily accessible ruins are of the Agora, in a fenced site just off the main road on the inland side. This was the market area and though it is a relatively small site many pillars are still visible, which make it quite an impressive place. Up a track from the Agora is the Acropolis and remains of a Temple to Aphrodite. There is evidence that some of the site lies underwater, which offers interesting opportunities for snorkellers and scuba-divers.

✚ 8B ✉ 8km (5 miles) east of Limassol ⏰ Apr–May, Sep–Oct daily 9–6; Jun–Aug daily 9–7.30; Nov–Mar daily 9–5 🎟 Inexpensive 🚌 From Limassol and Larnaka

CASTLE AND CYPRUS MEDIEVAL MUSEUM

The main buildings of the castle were constructed in the 14th century on the site of an earlier Byzantine fortification. The chapel in which Richard the Lionheart and Berengaria were married was part of the original castle but is no longer standing. The castle was occupied by the Turks and later used by the British as an army headquarters.

The Cyprus Medieval Museum is now housed here. The basement contains replicas of sculptures and photographs of the Byzantine churches of Cyprus. Upstairs the exhibits are in small rooms off a central hall, with the most memorable items – armour and weapons – on the second floor. The final flight of stairs leads

out on to the battlements, from where there are good views of the city. The most distinctive sights on the skyline are the two mosques, Cami Djedid and Cami Kebir, reminders that this was once the Turkish part of town.

✠ *Limassol 2a* ✉ Odos Eirinis, near the old harbour ☎ 2530 5419 ⏰ Mon–Sat 9–5, Sun 10–1. Closed 1 Jan, 25 Dec 💰 Inexpensive 🍴 Many cafés nearby (£)

DISTRICT ARCHAEOLOGICAL MUSEUM

The garden contains a sundial that supposedly belonged to the British Lord Kitchener. Inside, Room 1 contains neolithic tools and pottery from Amathous (➤ 104) and Kourion

(➤ 40–41). These artefacts are very old, with some dating back to 2300BC. Room 2 has later figurines and Roman coins. The final room contains statues from Amathous including those of Artemis and the Egyptian god Bes.

✠ *Limassol 4c* ✉ Corner of Odos Kanningos and Odos Vyronos ☎ 2530 5157 ⏰ Mon–Fri 10–5, Sat 10–1. Closed 1 Jan, 25 Dec, Greek Orthodox Easter Sun 💰 Inexpensive

MUNICIPAL GARDENS AND ZOO

The Municipal Gardens provide some welcome greenery in a dusty city. They also contain a small zoo, though the animals are kept in poor conditions. There is a small open-air theatre, where productions are held during the summer. The gardens are also the site of the annual Limassol Wine Festival, held in September. All the local wine companies set up stalls and have an evening of free wine tasting accompanied by music and dancing.

✚ *Limassol 4c* ✉ Odos Oktovriou 28 ☎ 2558 8345 🌐 Gardens: daylight hours. Zoo: daily 9–6.30 ✋ Gardens: free. Zoo: moderate 🍴 Café in the Gardens (£)

What to See in the Southwest

AKROTIRI PENINSULA

The area contains a good beach, a salt lake and a historic church. In summer the salt lake is dry, has a grey colour and you can smell the salt; in winter it fills with water and is a stopping off point for passing flamingos. Lady's Mile Beach is sandy and has safe swimming in the shallow sea. The far end is closed off, marking the start of the British base at Akrotiri – the occasional military jet may disturb the peace.

The monastery of **Agios Nikolaos ton Gaton** (St Nicholas of the Cats) is reached on a track at the southern end of the beach. It was founded in AD325, though the buildings seen today were constructed in the 13th century and have been restored since. The cats in the name are still much in evidence.

✚ 6A

Agios Nikolaos ton Gaton

🕐 Daily. Closed during mid-afternoon ✋ Free 🍴 Cafés on beach (£)

AVDIMOU BEACH

Avdimou Beach is a good long sandy stretch, though the water becomes deep very quickly. There is a small taverna at each end and it is usually quiet, but at weekends it can be busy with service personnel and their families. It is part of the British Sovereign Base and so has not seen any tourist development.

✚ 5A ✉ 3km (2 miles) off main road, opposite turning to Avdimou village 🍴 Taverna on beach (£)

CHOIROKOITIA

This is the oldest archaeological site on the island, dating
from 6800BC when 2,000 people lived here and farmed the
surrounding land.

The beehive-shape houses that define the settlement, come
in two sizes, one about 4m (13ft) across and the other 8m (26ft).
They were built close together and linked by narrow passageways, and it was apparently crowded. The inhabitants tended to
bury their dead under the floor of the house and then build on top,
and some houses have revealed up to eight different periods
of occupation.

The settlement is best explored by following the vestiges of

the main street,
with House A near
the entrance being
the easiest to make
out. A second group
of ruins has the
remains of pillars
visible which
once supported the
roof. From there the
site becomes more
complicated and the
best views are from

the top of the hill, from where the wider perspective can reveal
its layout.

➕ 9C ✉ Off Junction 14 Nicosia–Limassol motorway ☎ 2432 2710
🕐 Apr–May, Sep–Oct daily 9–6; Jun–Aug Mon–Fri 9–7.30, Sat–Sun 9–5;
Nov–Mar daily 9–5. Closed 1 Jan, 25 Dec, Greek Orthodox Easter Sun
✋ Inexpensive

GOVERNOR'S BEACH

See page 68.

KOLOSSI CASTLE

Kolossi was the headquarters of the Knights Hospitaller, who built the first castle in the late 13th century. They exploited the land here, using local sugar and grapes to make Commandaria wine.

The castle suffered from a number of attacks by Egyptian Mameluke raiders in the 14th century, and the buildings visible today date from a rebuilding that took place in the 15th century. The Turks took it over in 1570 and sugar production continued until 1799. Visitors pass over a drawbridge into a pleasant garden and then into the keep, which has thick wall and rises to three storeys.

Much of the ground floor was used as a storage area. The first floor has two large rooms and a kitchen. On the top floor were the apartments of the Grand Commander. A spiral staircase leads onto the roof, from where there are good views.

🚩 6B ✉ 14.5km (9 miles) from Limassol ☎ 2593 4907 🕐 Apr–May, Sep–Oct daily 9–6; Jun–Aug daily 9–7.30; Nov–Mar daily 9–5 💷 Inexpensive 🍴 Cafés nearby (£–££)

KOURION

See pages 40–41.

LEFKARA

The village is divided into Pano (upper) and Kato (lower) Lefkara, and is a very popular tourist destination. Visitors who prefer to avoid the crowds come in the early morning.

Lefkara is known for its lace, called *lefkaritika*; it first became famous in 1481 when Leonardo da Vinci supposedly ordered some for Milan Cathedral. The lace then became popular with Venetian ladies and the lacemaking industry took off. The tradition continues to flourish and rather ferocious ladies will offer their wares vigorously to passing tourists. Those wishing to buy should take care to ensure that it is the genuine article and not imported. There are also a number of silverware shops.

The main street of Pano Lefkara is now designed to cater for tourists but the narrow alleys to either side are still peaceful places to wander. There is also a small **museum** of lacemaking and silverware, signposted uphill from the main street.

The lower half of the village is often neglected but is worth a visit. Its church of Archangel Michael has some beautiful 18th-century icons and there are good views across the hills from outside the building. The distinctive houses in this part of the village are painted blue and white and its streets are extremely narrow and therefore traffic free.

➕ 9C ✉ 9km (5.5 miles) northwest of junction 13 of the Nicosia–Limassol motorway 🍴 Cafés in the main street of the upper village (£)

Museum

☎ 2434 2326 🕐 Mon–Thu 9.30–4, Fri–Sat 10–4
✋ Inexpensive

PETRA TOU ROMIOU (ROCK OF APHRODITE)

This is one of the most photographed sites on the whole island. The name means the Rock of Romios and the two large rocks in the sea, set against the white cliffs, provide a spectacular scene. There are two official places to stop – one close to the rock, just back from the shore, where there is a café and a car park, the other higher up in the cliffs, where there is a tourist pavilion. However, the best view, coming from Limassol, is on the final bend before the road starts to descend; some scrubland on the left makes a convenient stopping place.

Legend states that this was the birthplace of Aphrodite, where she emerged from the water. The beach itself is shingly, and it is not ideal for swimming because it gets rough around the rocks, but it is worth stopping to soak up the mysterious atmosphere.
➕ 3B ✉ 24km (15 miles) east of Pafos 🍴 Two cafés, one in the tourist pavilion (£)

SANCTUARY OF APOLLO YLATIS

The temple was first used in the 8th century BC, though the present ruins date from AD100, when it was rebuilt after an earthquake. There is a waymarked path and map to guide the visitor around the site. The circular remains of a votive pit are worth a closer look. The pit was used to store unwanted ritual gifts and archaeologists have found it a rich source of artefacts. The path then leads to the Temple of Apollo, which has been partially restored, its high columns a striking reminder of ancient times. A shed structure covers the Priest's House, and though you have to peer through the fence you can see some mosaics and pillars.

The remaining buildings of interest are the Palaestra, which was an open space used for sporting activities, and a nearby complex of baths.

✚ 5B ✉ Limassol–Pafos road ☎ 2599 7049 🕐 Apr–May, Sep–Oct daily 9–6; Jun–Aug daily 9–7.30; Nov–Mar daily 9–5. Closed 1 Jan, 25 Dec, Greek Orthodox Easter Sun ✋ Inexpensive

HOTELS

LIMASSOL (LEMESOS)

Amathus Beach (£££)

Opulent and with fine gardens it is situated by the shore at the eastern end of the tourist strip.

✉ Leoforos Amathus ☎ 2583 2000; www.amathushotel.com

Atlantica Bay (££)

Enjoys an elevated position close to ancient Amathous.

✉ Leoforos Amathus ☎ 2563 4070; www.atlanticahotels.com

Curium Palace (£)

An older style hotel in the town and one which has maintained high standards over the years. The antique furniture and friendly owner add to the atmosphere. Dining options are first class.

✉ 11 Odos Lordou Vyronou ☎ 2589 1100; www.curiumpalace.com

Four Seasons (£££)

The hotel enjoys a good reputation. Interior finishes are high quality and the swimming pool is excellent. Thalassotherapy and seaweed treatments are among the facilities on offer.

✉ Leoforos Amathus ☎ 2585 8000; www.fourseasons.com.cy

Le Meridien Limassol Spa & Resort (£££)

See page 77.

Miramare (££)

This hotel was built long before Limassol's coastal strip grew into a continuous ribbon of development. It became popular with the British over the years, not least because of the excellent service.

✉ Odos Amerikanas, Potamos Germasogeias ☎ 2588 8100; www.miramare.com.cy

Sunsmile (£)

On a narrow side street, but with parking, this is a good low budget choice. The apartments are self-catering but basic. Inexpensive good meals are available in the dining room. In the

central courtyard the moderate sized pool is fine for cooling off.
Reception and staff are friendly.
✉ 5 Odos Xenofanous ☎ 2532 0700

PISSOURI
Bunch of Grapes Inn (£)
A restored old inn and pleasant courtyard with 11 guest rooms;
quite different from the modern hotels.
✉ 9 Odos Ioannou Erotokritou, Pissouri village ☎ 2522 1275

Hylatio Tourist Village (£)
These pleasing studios and apartments with pool do not have a
sea view but it is only a short walk to the beach. A car would
enhance a quiet holiday.
✉ Pissouri Beach area ☎ 2522 2701

Pissouriana Plaza Apartments (£)
Reasonably spacious apartments with tremendous views. There
is a swimming pool.
✉ Pissouri village ☎ 2522 1027; www.pissouriana.com

RESTAURANTS
LIMASSOL (LEMESOS)
Barolo (£££)
This converted old house with a garden is a delightful place to
enjoy some quality modern Mediterranean cuisine and a huge
wine selection.
✉ 248 Odos Agiou Andreou ☎ 2576 0767 🕐 Mon–Sat 7–11

Karatello (££–£££)
An old carob warehouse close to the Cami Kebir mosque has been
transformed into a chic modern eatery, where traditional Cypriot
and Mediterranean dishes are given a *nouvelle* touch.
✉ Odos Vasilissis ☎ 2582 0430 🕐 Daily

Ladas Old Harbour Fish Restaurant (££)
The fish comes straight from the boats in the adjacent harbour to

this restaurant, which has been here for more than 50 years.
It reaches your plate with the minimum of delay.

✉ Old Harbour ☎ 2536 5760 🕘 Daily

La Mer (£)

A good place for lunch if you have just done the Limassol walk
(➤ 72–73).

✉ Elpa Court, Odos Oktovriou 28, just west of Municipal Gardens ☎ 2535
6095 🕘 Daily

Mamas (£££)

It is a pleasure to eat here, the menu is extensive and a high
professional standard is maintained throughout.

✉ Kanika Panorama Court, Leoforos Amathountas, towards Elena Beach
Hotel ☎ 2532 3433 🕘 Daily

Meze Taverna Restaurant (££)

This family restaurant is a transplant from St Albans, in the UK,
and it has travelled well, with lovely Greek Cypriot food including
an excellent *meze*, along with fish and vegetarian dishes.

✉ 209 Odos Agiou Andreou ☎ 2536 7333 🕘 Mon–Sat 12–3, 6–11

Pallio Varka (££)

In an interesting old building, this restaurant has a varied menu
including excellent Greek dishes.

✉ 1 Odos Vasilisis, opposite the castle ☎ 2534 7171 🕘 Daily

Porta (££)

Something more atmospheric than this restaurant in a converted
donkey stable in the old centre would be hard to imagine, but the
conversion works well, and the Cypriot standbys on the menu are
joined by a popular Mongolian dish!

✉ 17 Odos Genethliou Mitella ☎ 2536 0339 🕘 Daily

Prima Italian Restaurant (££)

Modern and colourful, well-presented Italian fare.

✉ 139 Odos Agiou Andreou ☎ 2576 3076 🕘 Daily

Xydas (£££)

A top-notch restaurant serving fresh fish dishes.
✉ 22 Odos Anthemidos, Amathous ☎ 2572 8336 🕐 Daily

PISSOURI
Bunch of Grapes Inn (££)

Originally the village manor house the building is splendid and unique. The menu features a blend of traditional Cypriot dishes with the best of British and French cuisine.
✉ Pissouri Village ☎ 2522 1275 🕐 Daily

ZYGI
Markos (££)

A reliable taverna serving freshly caught fish right on the seafront.
✉ Village seafront ☎ 2433 3404 🕐 Daily

SHOPPING

JEWELLERY
Precious Metal Gallery

Beautifully crafted gold, silver and enamel jewellery.
✉ Agora Anexartisias, Odos Agiou Andreou, Limassol ☎ 2535 3639

SOUVENIRS, LEATHER AND HANDICRAFTS
Artouch

Paintings, sculptures, ceramics and hand-crafted jewellery.
✉ 29 Odos Agiou Andreou, Limassol ☎ 2576 2660

Cyprus Handicraft Service

Cypriot handicrafts made in Government-run workshops.
✉ 25 Odos Themidos, Limassol ☎ 2530 5118

House of Lace

Large selection of Lefkara lace.
✉ 143 Odos Agiou Andreou, Limassol ☎ 2536 5040

Kingdom of Leather

✉ 43 Odos Georgiou A', Potamos, Germasogeias, Limassol ☎ 2535 3271

Lefkara Village
A wide range of silverware and lace on sale in the village (► 112).
Check that you are buying a genuine article, not an import.

Sea Sponge Exhibition Centre
Natural beauty products, including soaps and loofahs.
✉ Old Port, Limassol ☎ 2535 9933

STORES AND ARCADES
Agora
An impressive modern arcade. Some quality clothes and footwear
outlets along with a unique jewellery gallery.
✉ Junction of Odos Agiou Andreou and Odos Anexartisias, Limassol

Anexartisia Shopping Street
Has around 160 shops. Although some outlets might close, the
Street is here to stay and worth a visit.
✉ Odos Anexartisias, Limassol

Debenhams
The standard range of department store goods.
✉ 27 Odos Oktovriou 28, Limassol ☎ 2559 1133

Medieval Arcade
Mainly restaurants and cafés, but including a bookshop.
✉ West end of Odos Agiou Andreou, Limassol

ENTERTAINMENT AND SPORT

THEATRE AND CULTURAL EVENTS
Ancient Greek Drama Festival (June–August)
Performances of classical drama are held in the amphitheatre at
Kourion and other open-air theatres in the area.

Limassol Festival
Limassol Municipality organizes theatre, music and dance events
throughout the summer.
☎ 2536 3103 for information

HORSE-BACK RIDING
Amathus Park Riding School
✉ Near Parekklisia, Highway junction 21 ☎ 9960 4109

Drapia Farm
✉ Kalavasos, 30km (18.5 miles) east of Limassol ☎ 2433 2998

Elias Beach Country Club
✉ Near Parekklisia, 10km (6 miles) northeast of Limassol ☎ 2563 6000

Mouttayiaki Ranch
✉ Just north of Highway junction 23, Limassol ☎ 9943 7515

SAILING
Cyprus Yachting Association
✉ PO Box 51813, 3508 Limassol ☎ 2532 0599; www.cya.org.cy

Relax Catamaran Cruises
Sailing from Limassol Old Port to Cape Gata, various permutations
of time, distance and price.
☎ 8000 8007; 9956 2074

St Raphael Marina
Visiting yachtsmen and -women can use the facilities of the
St Raphael Hotel.
✉ Limassol ☎ 2563 5800

TEN-PIN BOWLING
Limassol Bowling
✉ Odos Argyrokastrou, Limassol ☎ 2537 0414 🕐 2pm–midnight

Space Bowling
✉ 1 Odos Hercule Germasogeia, motorway junction 23 area ☎ 2531 0000
🕐 Daily 10am–2am

Pafos and the West

This is the region for those looking for some of Cyprus's quieter and more traditional areas. However, Pafos (Paphos) continues to expand greatly and has cast off its small town origins, although not its important archaeological heritage. In the north are monasteries and villages. Polis, the only town of any size on the north coast, is no longer as laid-back as it once was. In the far northwest is the Akamas peninsula, which is the focus of environmental initiatives to protect some of the most remote and beautiful landscapes in Cyprus. East of Polis is an undeveloped region with empty beaches and quiet roads up to the Green Line that marks the limit of easy exploration for visitors in the Greek Cypriot sector of the island.

Pafos (Paphos)

The first settlement dates from the 4th century BC and Pafos played an important role in early Cypriot history. After the 4th century AD it declined and, though its fortunes improved marginally under British administration, it is only in the last 30 years, as transport links improved, that Pafos has seen real growth. Tourist development, in particular, took off after the construction of the international airport in 1983. The richness of its archaeology has qualified ancient Nea Pafos as a UNESCO World Heritage Site.

The town is split into upper and lower Pafos, known as Kitma and Kato Pafos. The lower part, on the coast, contains most of the historic sites whereas the upper town contains the main commercial centre, shops and modern museums. It is quite a strenuous walk between the two parts of town. The lower town contains a number of archaeological sites. Some are in formal areas, but you might come across ancient ruins among modern houses. The harbour is the focus of the lower town and is a pleasant place to stroll. Cafés string out along the seafront and there are plenty of places to eat or have a drink, although it can be very busy at the height of the season.

 2C

CATACOMBS

There are two underground churches in Pafos. Agia Solomoni is easily identified because those who believe in the magical curative powers of the tomb attach items of clothing to the tree outside.

The underground chambers include a 12th-century chapel with frescoes, some of which are damaged by water and early graffiti by passing crusaders. The chambers are dark and a torch is useful, though the main chapel is lit by candles.

The second catacomb, a few minutes walk north, is larger, but has been less well cared for.

➕ *Pafos 2c* ✉ Leoforos Apostolou Pavlou 🕐 Daylight hours ✋ Free

DISTRICT ARCHAEOLOGICAL MUSEUM

The museum houses most of the finds from local excavations. In the entrance hall is a Hellenistic sarcophagus from Pegeia and there are pottery and terracotta figures from Polis. There are also small statues and artefacts from the House of Dionysos, and sculpture and coins from the ancient city kingdoms of Cyprus. Most fascinating are articles found in Room 3, including marble Roman eyeballs and clay hot-water bottles.

➕ *Pafos 4d* ✉ Leoforos Georgiou Griva Digeni ☎ 2630 6215 🕐 Mon–Fri 9–4, Sat–Sun 9–1. Closed 1 Jan, 25 Dec, Greek Orthodox Easter Sun ✋ Inexpensive 🍴 Cafés across the road (£)

ETHNOGRAPHICAL MUSEUM

This private collection of George Eliades, a local professor, ranges from neolithic to modern times. The collection includes axe heads, coins, pottery and farm implements from around the island. There is also a reconstruction of a bridal chamber displaying traditional costumes and furniture.

➕ *Pafos 3d* ✉ 1 Odos Exo Vrisis ☎ 2693 2010 🕐 Mar–Nov Mon–Sat 9–5, Sun 10–1; Dec–Feb Mon–Sat 9.30–5, Sun 10–1 ✋ Inexpensive 🍴 Cafés nearby (£)

ODEION

This theatre has been partially restored to give an impression of how it would once have been. It was built in the 2nd century AD, during the Roman period, then suffered earthquake damage in the 7th century and was abandoned. Occasional performances are held here during the summer and details are available from the tourist office. Just in front of the Odeion is the Agora, once the city's market place. The foundations and some of the columns survive, and there are remains of some other municipal buildings.

➕ *Pafos 1c* ✉ Within the World Heritage Site, a short distance inland from the harbour ⏰ Jun–Aug daily 8–7.30; Sep–May daily 8–5 ✋ Moderate, including Mosaics and Saranda Kolones 🍴 Cafés (£) nearby

PAFOS FORT

Originally the harbour was guarded by two castles built by the
Lusignans in the 13th century. Both were badly damaged when
the Turks attacked in 1570, but one was subsequently restored
and used by the Turks as a prison. It is open to the public and you
approach across a drawbridge. The main attractions are the
dungeons and battlements, from where there are excellent views.
🔁 *Pafos 1b* ✉ Harbour Wall ☎ 2693 2841 🕐 Jun–Aug daily 10–6;
Sep–May daily 10–5. Closed 1 Jan, 25 Dec, Greek Orthodox Easter Sun
✋ Inexpensive 🍴 Cafés on harbour front (££)

PAFOS MOSAICS

See pages 48–49.

ST PAUL'S PILLAR AND AGIA KYRIAKI

This is a small archaeological site in
the back streets of Pafos, where a
large number of columns and other
fragments remain from the early
Christian Basilica of Agia Kyriaki.
Excavations are still taking place and
this may mean that parts of the site
will be closed off. Most people come
here to see St Paul's Pillar, which
stands at the western end of the
site. According to legend, St Paul was tied to this stone and given
39 lashes as a punishment for preaching Christianity. Despite this
early setback, he later managed to convert the governor, and the
rest of the island soon followed suit.

The adjacent church of Panagia Chrysopolitissa dates from
the 12th century and is still used for services.
🔁 *Pafos 2b* ✉ Odos Stassandrou 🕐 Daylight hours ✋ Free
🍴 Cafés nearby (£)

SARANDA KOLONES (FORTY COLUMNS) BYZANTINE FORT

This castle dates from around the 7th century, although it was rebuilt in the 12th century, probably to protect the city from seaborne raiders until it was replaced by the forts on the breakwater. The remains of many of the original columns, the central keep and some of the towers on the thick outer walls can still be made out. You can also see a horse-trough and ancient latrines. The site is completely open and you can scramble around the ruins, but take care if you have young children.

✚ *Pafos 2b* ✉ Within the World Heritage Site, a short distance from the harbour 🕓 Jun–Aug daily 8–7.30; Sep–May daily 8–5 ✋ Moderate, including mosaics and Odeion 🍴 Cafés nearby (££)

TAFON TON VASILEON (TOMBS OF THE KINGS)

The 100 tombs on the site cover a wide area and are cut out of the ground with a steep drop into them, so take care when exploring. Steps lead down inside the tombs, often into a whole series of passageways. The chambers near the centre of the site get busy and it is worth walking a little further to those on the edge of the area, which are just as impressive. They are constructed with Doric columns, date from about the 3rd century BC and were probably used to bury members of local noble families.

There are some good views over the sea and a few coves are accessible.

✚ *Pafos 1e* ✉ Leoforos Tafon ton Vasileon, 2km (1 mile) northwest of Pafos ☎ 2630 6295 🕓 Apr–May, Sep–Oct daily 8–6; Jun–Aug daily 8–7.30; Nov–Mar daily 8–5 ✋ Inexpensive 🍴 Café on site (£) 🚌 10, 15 from Pafos

What to See in the West

AGIOS GEORGIOS

Agios Georgios is a pleasant harbour with a handful of restaurants, a small cluster of hotels and rooms to rent. The whole area was once a Roman settlement and some of the tombs cut out of the rock can be seen. On the headland are the remains of a 6th-century basilica.

The harbour is reached down a track from the headland and signposted Mandoulis beach. It is a very pretty place with a good stretch of sand and a view to the rocky island of Geronisos.

🔶 1D ✉ 25km (15.5 miles) north of Pafos 🍴 Restaurants overlooking the harbour (£)

AGIOS NEOFYTOS MONASTERY

Saint Neofytos set up residence in caves he cut out of the hillside in 1159. The first cave he created was called the *enkleistra*, or enclosure. He then enlarged the dwelling with the addition of three new chambers, which are decorated with religious wall paintings focusing on the Crucifixion and Resurrection. Those in the sanctuary, the cave with an altar, are the best preserved. The 16th-century monastery church is dedicated to the Virgin Mary and contains a large number of paintings that depict her early life. Neofytos's bones are also kept here in a wooden sarcophagus, with his skull in a silver reliquary, which the devoted queue up to kiss.

🔶 2C ✉ 9km (5.5 miles) north of Pafos 🕐 Apr–Oct daily 9–12, 2–4; Nov–Mar daily 9–4 💰 Inexpensive 🍴 Café outside monastery 🚌 Two buses a day from Pafos lower town

AKAMAS PENINSULA

See pages 36–37.

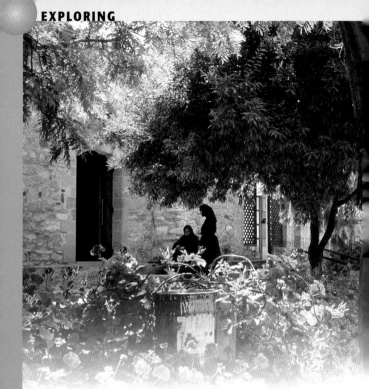

CHRYSORROGIATISSA MONASTERY

The monastery is impressive mainly because of its setting at a height of 610m (2,000ft). It was founded in 1152 by a monk called Ignatius, although the main part of the monastery was not built until 1770. These buildings were burned down in 1821 when the Turks suspected the monks of political activity. Further trouble came in the 1950s when the abbot was murdered by EOKA terrorists who thought, erroneously, he had betrayed some of their comrades.

The current abbot has shown much enterprise in reopening an old winery and the monks now produce and sell some excellent wines. A collection of icons and utensils are displayed in an area called the Treasury. Icons, painted by the abbot, are also for sale.

✚ 3D ✉ 3km (2 miles) south of (Pano) Panagia ☎ 2672 2457

🕐 Daily 9–sunset. Treasury: closed 12.30–1.30 ✋ Free.
Treasury: inexpensive 🍴 Café outside monastery (£)

CORAL BAY
See page 68.

GEROSKIPOU
The church of Agia Paraskevi, in the centre of the
village, is famous throughout the island because
of its distinctive five-domed plan. The building
dates from the 10th-century but it has a number
of decorations over the altar from the 9th century.
The paintings are slightly later, from the 12th to
the 15th century.

   There is also a good Folk Art Museum, just off
the main street, which contains farming and
domestic implements and traditional costumes.
The village is known for its *Loukoumi* ('Cyprus
delight', called 'Turkish delight' before the Turkish
invasion); it is possible to watch it being made in
some of the shops.

✚ 2B ✉ 3km (2 miles) east of Pafos ☎ Agia Paraskevi: 2696 1859.
Art Museum: 2630 6216 🕐 Church: Apr–Oct Mon–Sat 8–1, 2–5; Nov–Mar
Mon–Sat 8–1, 2–4, Sun 10–1. Folk Art Museum: Mon–Wed, Fri 9–2.30, Thu
9–2.30, 3–5. Closed
afternoons Jul–Aug
✋ Church: free. Folk
Art Museum:
inexpensive 🚌 From
Pafos old town

LARA
See pages 44–45.

PALAIA PAFOS (OLD PAFOS)/KOUKLIA

The site, on which stands the Sanctuary of Aphrodite, is spread over a large area. At the entrance is a restored Lusignan manor (La Covocle) with substantial and impressive Turkish additions. In its main hall is a museum with exhibits focusing on the history of the excavation of the area and the fragments of mosaic that have been found. Its prize possession is a large black stone that stood as a manifestation of Aphrodite and was worshipped by pilgrims. The hall itself is worth a closer look as it is one of the best examples of 13th-century Gothic architecture on the island.

To the east of the museum are Roman remains, including remnants of the Sanctuary of Aphrodite, which stands around a courtyard where rituals took place. The south wing is the best preserved, and parts of the original walls still stand.

West of the sanctuary are the ruins of Roman houses, including the House of Leda; follow the path that leads to a replica of a mosaic of Leda and the Swan.

✚ 3B 🖂 14km (8.5 miles) east of Pafos ☎ 2643 2180 🕓 Daily 9–4. Closed 1 Jan, 25 Dec, Greek Orthodox Easter Sun ✋ Museum: inexpensive. Rest of the site: free

PANAGIA

The village of (Pano) Panagia is the place where Archbishop Makarios was born. Makarios played a key role in the campaign for independence from the British and he was the first president of Cyprus from independence in 1960 until his death in 1977.

His parents' house in the village is now a museum. It consists of two rooms, with his parents' bed, assorted crockery and family photographs. If nothing else, the house shows that Archbishop Makarios had a humble background. In the main square is a cultural centre, which displays more photographs and memorabilia from his later life as president.

✚ 4D 🖂 (Pano) Panagia village centre 🕓 Cultural Centre: May–Sep daily 9–1, 3–6; Oct–Apr daily 9–1, 2–4. Makarios's House: daily 9–2, 2–4
✋ Cultural Centre: free. Makarios's House: donation requested 🍴 Many cafés in village (£)

POLIS

The town has traditionally been a destination for backpackers and other more unconventional travellers. Most of the main restaurants and shops are found around a pedestrianised square, with a number of rooms and apartments to rent close by. There is a good beach a short walk from the town centre, with a campsite adjacent.

Just east of the town, but difficult to identify, is the ancient site of Marion, which was founded in the 7th century BC and developed into one of the 10 city kingdoms of Cyprus.

➕ 2E

POMOS

There are some wonderful quiet beaches along this section of coast, and as the road climbs up into the cliffs there are amazing views. Just beyond Pomos Point is a small fishing harbour and sheltered beach. Kokkina is occupied by the Turkish army and is inaccessible. The road detours inland and then reaches Kato Pyrgos where there is another isolated beach.

➕ 3F ✉ 22km (13.5 miles) northwest of Polis 🍴 Cafés at Kato Pyrgos (£) 🚌 Limited bus service from Polis to Pomos, at 11, 2, 4, 6; Sat 11, 2.30, 4

HOTELS

Agapinor (£)
Well-appointed rooms (73) plus restaurant and coffee shop.
Remarkable views.
✉ 24–28 Odos Nikodimou Mylona, Pafos ☎ 2693 3926;
www.agapinorhotel.com.cy

Akamanthea Tourist Village (££)
Excellent small complex in wonderful surroundings. Self catering,
but there are lots of facilities, a swimming pool and a central area.
✉ Lakki, near Polis ☎ 2632 3500; www.akamanthea.com

Almyra (£££)
Enviable shore location 600m (650yds) from harbour.
✉ Leoforos Poseidonos, Kato Pafos ☎ 2693 3091; www.thanoshotels.com

Aloe (££)
This well-run hotel is near the shore and the amenities of Kato
Pafos.
✉ Leoforos Poseidonos, Kato Pafos ☎ 2696 4000; www.aloe-hotel.com.cy

Annabelle (£££)
A renowed luxury hotel in a prime position in town.
✉ Leoforos Poseidonos, Kato Pafos ☎ 2693 8333; www.thanoshotels.com

Atlantic Golden Beach (££)
A resort hotel beside a small beach.
✉ Kisonerga ☎ 2694 7777; www.atlanticahotels.com

Cynthiana Beach (£££)
This hotel has a combination of resort hotel facilities and
reasonable isolation just 7km (4 miles) north of Pafos itself. Also
has a small private beach.
✉ Kisonerga ☎ 2693 3900; www.cynthianahotel.com

Cyprotel Droushia Heights (££)
Perched on an eyrie in the hills this hotel is away from everything.

Without a car a stay here will be exceedingly quiet. A thick
sweater is needed for the cool evenings of early and late summer.
The view over Chrysochou Bay is terrific.

✉ Drouseia ☎ 2633 2351; www.dhcyprotels.com

Leptos Coral Beach (£££)

Large hotel adjacent to the beach at Coral Bay. Facilities include
indoor and outdoor swimming pools. The popular beach can get
very busy.

✉ Coral Bay ☎ 2688 1000; www.coral.com.cy

Park Mansion (£–££)

See page 77.

Souli (£)

Comfortable, simply furnished rooms in a quiet hotel. There is an
outdoor pool. The seafood restaurant is excellent.

✉ Lakki–Neo Chorio road ☎ 2632 1088

RESTAURANTS

PAFOS (PAPHOS)
Argo (££)

Their claim to produce the best *meze* in town seems eminently
reasonable after you have sampled it.

✉ 21 Odos Pafias Afroditis, Kato Pafos ☎ 2623 3327 🕓 Daily

Cavallini (£££)

A fount of tasteful modern Italian cuisine, with a stylishly rustic
interior and an outside terrace that sufffers from being a bit too
close to a busy main street.

✉ 65 Leoforos Poseidonos, Kato Pafos ☎ 2696 4164 🕓 Mon–Sat
6pm–midnight

Deep Blue (££)

A well designed restaurant with a modern nautical feel to it.
Excellent seafood.

✉ 12 Odos Pafias Afroditis, Kato Pafos ☎ 2681 8015 🕓 Mon–Sat 6–11

Gina's Place (££)

Bistro-cafe and wine bar serving gourmet sandwiches and salads with superior imported wines. An adjacent delicatessen counter stocks a wide range of foods.

✉ 3 Odos Agiou Antoniou, Kato Pafos ☎ 2693 8017 ◷ Mon–Sat 9am–11pm (summer), 9–7 (winter)

Kings Aphrodite Restaurant (££)

Greek restaurant offering excellent *souvlaki*, suckling pig and all the usual Greek fare. Music several nights a week.

✉ Leoforos Tafon Ton Vasileon, 300m (330yds) after traffic lights, Kato Pafos ☎ 2694 1917 ◷ Daily

Pelican (£–££)

Few visitors can resist dining at Pafos's scenic harbour, but not many of the waterfront eateries justify their hopes. Pelican is a decent but not notable performer across the range of Cypriot food.

✉ 102 Leoforos Apostolou Pavlou, Kato Pafos ☎ 2694 6886 ◷ Daily

Seagull (££)

Close to the shore. A varied menu, efficient service and good atmosphere make for a most enjoyable meal.

✉ 7 Leoforos Poseidonos, Kato Pafos ☎ 2695 0489 ◷ Daily

Ta Mpavia (££)

Well-designed and in a good position by the sea. The food is pretty good too.

✉ Seafront, Leoforos Poseidonos, Kato Pafos ☎ 2694 1558 ◷ Daily

POLIS-LAKKI AREA

Baths of Aphrodite (££)

Simple taverna serving good fish.

✉ Opposite Baths of Aphrodite trail start ☎ 2632 1457 ◷ Daily

Central Point (£)

A good lunch stop, prompt service and modest prices.

✉ Polis Square ☎ 2632 1800 ◷ Daily

Finikas (££)
Ideal for alfresco dining with a varied menu.

✉ Polis Square ☎ 2632 3403 🕐 Daily (Dec–Feb snacks only)

Moustakallis Tavern Restaurant (££)
Family-run, with an excellent choice of Cypriot food.

✉ Off the south side of Polis Square ☎ 2632 2883 🕐 Daily

Seafare Restaurant (££)
The proprietor is charming and the seafood second to none. The wonderful harbour setting is a bonus.

✉ Lakki Harbour, west of Polis ☎ 2632 2274

SHOPPING

JEWELLERY
Athos Diamond Centre
Exclusive agents for many of the big names.

✉ 79–80 Leoforos Poseidonos, Kato Pafos ☎ 2681 1630

SOUVENIRS, HANDICRAFTS AND LEATHER
Cyprus Handicraft Service
A wide selection of traditional Cypriot handicrafts made in Government-run workshops.

✉ 64 Leoforos Apostolou Pavlou, Kato Pafos ☎ 2630 6243

Fyti Village
The villagers produce fine woven cloth, especially embroidered curtains.

Mavris Leather House
Leather garments off the peg or made to measure.

✉ 5 Odos Dionysou, Kato Pafos ☎ 2693 5646

Mosaics Plaza
Unique gifts and souvenirs in gold and silver, plus mineral and gemstone items. Also a section of leather goods.

✉ Harbour, Kato Pafos ☎ 2681 9999

STORES AND ARCADES
Debenhams
A very smart department store.
✉ Odos Lidras, Kato Pafos ☎ 2694 7122

ENTERTAINMENT AND SPORTS

CULTURAL EVENTS
Pafos Aphrodite Festival
Pafos Municipality organizes theatre, music and dance events in
September at the Odeion Roman theatre and the harbour fort.
☎ 2682 2218

GOLF
Aphrodite Hills
18-hole course, set in the grounds of a 12th-century monastery in
a valley. Facilities include a restaurant, tennis and outdoor pool.
✉ North of Pafos ☎ 2681 8700

Secret Valley
18-hole course, set in a scenic valley surrounded by rock
formations.
✉ East of Pafos, near Petra tou Romiou ☎ 2664 2774

Tsada Golf Club
✉ Tsada, 12km (7.5 miles) northeast of Pafos ☎ 2664 2774

HORSE-BACK RIDING
George's Ranch
✉ Agios Georgios, 20km (12.5 miles) north of Pafos ☎ 2662 1064

TEN-PIN BOWLING
Cockatoos
✉ Odos Agiou Antoniou, Kato Pafos ☎ 2682 2004 ⏰ Daily 10–3

Nicosia and The High Troodos

Nicosia (Lefkosia) lies inland on the Mesaoria, or central plain. This location allowed the city to avoid the devastation wreaked on the coastal towns by Arab raiders. Here the plain is relatively narrow, with the Pentadaktylos Mountains to the north and the foothills of the Troodos approaching the city from the southwest.

The northern boundary is no arbitrary choice: the Green Line that still divides Cyprus cuts through the heart of Nicosia. But visitors will now find it a frontier they can cross at several points in Nicosia as well as elsewhere along its length.

To the south is a splendid area of valleys and villages; Stavros tis Psokas in the west is a lonely forest station; Machairas Monastery and its surrounding hills make up the eastern extremity.

Nicosia (Lefkosia)

NICOSIA

Despite the opening of the border, Nicosia, the capital of Cyprus, remains a divided city. The border, known as the Green Line, separates the Greek Cypriot and Turkish Cypriot parts of the island and runs through the middle of the city. The Greek Cypriot side has all the hallmarks of a modern westernized place and is a thriving shopping and business centre, though its ancient history is visible. The Turkish Cypriot sector has a more dilapidated and Eastern feel, with narrower streets and old-fashioned shops.

Nicosia is always busy and is always hotter than the coast, so summer visitors should not plan too strenuous a programme. Fortunately the main attractions are within the old city walls and can be explored on foot. The walls themselves, built by the Venetians, still impress.

An extensive modernization and refurbishment programme is underway in the old part of town. The traffic-free Laïki Geitonia area is the most obvious result of that programme; it is a pleasant place to wander, with all the facilities a tourist could need, and

leads into some of the older shopping streets.

There is less to see in northern Nicosia and the narrow streets make it easy to get lost. However, almost all roads eventually lead to the main sight, the Selimiye Mosque, once the Cathedral of Santa Sophia, the minarets of which dominate this part of town. There are a number of other mosques in the vicinity, plus a few small museums and, for the more adventurous, the Turkish Baths.

 16J

Greek Cypriot Nicosia

AGIOS IOANNIS CATHEDRAL

The cathedral lies within the episcopal precinct and was built in 1662 on the site of a Benedictine abbey church. It contains some fine 18th-century wall paintings and is ornately decorated throughout. It is claimed that it contained the finger of St John the Baptist until it was stolen by Mameluke raiders. The cathedral is smaller than one might expect of a building of importance and is best visited early.

✚ *Nicosia 3d* ✉ Plateia Archiepiskopou Kyprianou 🕐 Mon–Fri 8–12, 2–4, Sat 8–12 👆 Free 🍽 Cafés nearby (£)

ARCHBISHOP MAKARIOS CULTURAL CENTRE (BYZANTINE MUSEUM)

The most important exhibits in the museum are the 6th-century Kanakaria Mosaics, which were thought lost when they were stolen from their church on the Karpasia peninsula in northern Cyprus. They were recovered when offered for sale on the international art market and were returned to this purpose-built wing of the museum. Also on show are a large number of icons from churches around the island.

✚ *Nicosia 3d* ✉ Plateia Archiepiskopou Kyprianou ☎ 2243 0008 ⏰ Mon–Fri 9–4.30, Sat 9–1 👋 Moderate 🍴 Cafés nearby (£)

CYPRUS MUSEUM

The museum houses most of the important finds from sites across Cyprus – neolithic artefacts, Bronze Age vases and clay figurines, Mycenaean objects from Kourion (➤ 40–41) and sophisticated pottery. Two thousand figurines found at Agia Irini are displayed as they were found, gathered around a single altar. A wide range of sculptures are on show, as well as a huge bronze statue of Roman Emperor Septimius Severus and the famous horned god from Enkomi. There are impressive items from Salamis (➤ 52–53), some mosaics and a reconstructed rock-cut tomb.

✚ *Nicosia 1d* ✉ Leoforos Mouseiou ☎ 2286 5888 ⏰ Mon–Sat 9–5, Sun 10–1. Closed 1 Jan, 25 Dec, Greek Orthodox Easter Sun 👋 Moderate 🍴 Café opposite (££)

FAMAGUSTA GATE

This was the main entrance into the old city from the south and east. It is set into the historic walls and has been restored to house a cultural centre that is used for exhibitions and other events. Artists have set up studios in old buildings in the area.

✚ *Nicosia 4e* ✉ Leoforos Athinon ☎ 2243 0877 🕐 Mon–Fri 10–1, 4–7, (5–8 Jun–Aug) 🖐 Free 🍴 Cafés nearby (£)

HADJIGEORGAKIS KORNESIOS HOUSE (ETHNOGRAPHICAL MUSEUM)

This house belonged to the grand dragoman of Cyprus, Hadjigeorgakis Kornesios, at the end of the 18th century. The dragoman was an interlocutor between the ethnic Greek and Turkish populations, an important and powerful role at that time. The museum contains a number of artefacts from the dragoman's life, displayed in reconstructions of some of the original rooms, along with letters and documents prepared by Kornesios.

✚ *Nicosia 3d* ✉ Odos Patriarchou Grigoriou ☎ 2230 5316 🕐 Mon–Fri 9–5.30 🖐 Inexpensive 🍴 Cafés nearby (£)

LAÏKI GEITONIA

This is a revived traffic-free area of old Nicosia where traditional buildings have been restored, shops refurbished and trees planted. It is specifically aimed at the tourist, with a whole range of restaurants, craft shops and the tourist office, as well as a small jewellery museum.

The old shopping streets of Lidras and Onasagoras that lead out of the Laïki Geitonia area are also interesting places to wander. Rather more traditional shops are found on these streets and at their northern end are the sandbags that mark the Green Line.

✚ *Nicosia 2d* ✉ Within old city walls, northeast of Plateia Eleftherias ❚❙ Many cafés (££)

LEVENTIS MUNICIPAL MUSEUM OF NICOSIA

This museum, in Laïki Geitonia, is well set out and modest in size. Medieval finds, some of which were uncovered when the building was being restored, are in the basement. The first floor deals with the period 2300BC to the Turkish era and the ground floor covers the British colonial time as well as the city's recent history. The documentation from this later time is particularly interesting although the commentaries can be a little partisan.

✚ *Nicosia 2d* ✉ Odos Ippokratou ☎ 2266 1475 ⏰ Tue–Sun 10–4.30. Closed 1 Jan, 25 Dec, Greek Orthodox Easter Sun ♿ Free ❚❙ Café in basement (££)

OMERIYE MOSQUE

As with many of the city's mosques, this building was originally a church, converted in 1571 by Lala Mustafa Paşa, the occupying Turkish general. He believed that the visit of the Muslim prophet Omar should be commemorated, and as a result the minaret was added and the old Lusignan tombstones used to cover the floor. The mosque is still used as a place of worship.

✚ *Nicosia 3d* ✉ Odos Trikoupi ⏰ Any reasonable hour and when there is prayer ♿ Free, donation expected ❚❙ Cafés nearby (£)

Turkish Cypriot Nicosia (Lefkoşa)

BÜYÜK HAMAM

This was once the Church of St George, built in the 14th century and subsequently converted to a bathhouse by the Turks. The main room is domed, the floor well below street level. On Fridays only women are permitted inside, other days men only. Should it be locked, the café owner on the west side has the key.

➕ *Nicosia 2e* ✉ Mousa Orfenbey Sokağı 🕗 Jun–Sep daily 7.30–1, 4–6; Oct–May daily 8–1, 2–6 ✋ Free entry. Baths: moderate 🍴 Café next door (£)

BÜYÜK HAN

The building was commissioned in 1572 by Lala Mustafa Paşa, the first Ottoman governor of Cyprus. It was a simple inn, complete with stables and a wonderful little mosque in the courtyard. Perhaps the nadir of its fortunes was when it became Nicosia's central prison in 1893. Its days of neglect are now over – the Department of Antiquities has restored it, albeit as a museum, and it now houses small shops and cafés, as well as serving as a venue for occasional concerts.

➕ *Nicosia 2e* ✉ Arasta Sokağı 🕗 Mon, Wed–Thu 8–8, Tue and Fri 8–midnight, Sat 8–3 ✋ Inexpensive

LAPIDARY MUSEUM

The building, on two levels, was perhaps once the home of a wealthy Venetian family. Assorted wooden relics from mosques and churches display fine carving. In the courtyard is a random selection of Corinthian capitals, carved stone heads and a section of a beautiful rose window.

✚ *Nicosia 3e* ✉ Northeast of the Selimiye Mosque 🕓 Jun–Sep daily 9–2; Oct–May 9–1, 2–2.45. If locked, try custodian at the Library of Sultan Mahmut II across the road 🖐 Inexpensive

MEVLEVI TEKKE (ETHNOGRAPHICAL MUSEUM)

This was the home of the whirling dervishes, a sect founded in the 13th century. The rooms have a simple elegance, complete with a splendid minstrels' gallery looking down on where the dervishes, heads lowered in contemplation, would stretch out their arms and spin at ever increasing speed. In 1925 Kemal Atatürk forbade such dancing in an attempt to modernize Turkish culture. After 20 years the ruling was relaxed and the dance celebrated once more. To one side is a collection of costumes, wedding dresses and musical instruments.

✚ Nicosia 2f ✉ Girne Caddesi 🕓 Jun–Sep Mon–Fri 9–2; Oct–Mar daily 9–1, 2–4.45 💵 Moderate

SELIMIYE MOSQUE

This impressive building was a Christian masterpiece before conversion to a mosque of the Ottoman Turks, the most important in Cyprus. The elevations of magnificent windows, portals and buttresses are discordant; the reason – the soaring minarets. They are landmarks in the walled city, and their imposition on the west front by the Turks reflects the momentous events of 1570–71.

The original cathedral was started in 1209 and substantially completed 117 years later. In reality it was never quite finished, work carrying on long after the consecration.

Everything changed with the arrival of the Turks. All the overt Christian decoration of the cathedral was destroyed. Soon work was started on the minarets and the building became the Cathedral of Santa Sophia until the name was changed to the Selimiye Mosque in 1954.

✚ Nicosia 3e ✉ Selimiye Sokağı 🕓 Daily 💵 Free

What to See in the High Troodos

AGIOS IRAKLEIDIOS

The monastery was founded in the Byzantine era, and it is
dedicated to the saint who guided St Paul and St Barnabas to
nearby Tamassos during their missionary travels. St Irakleidios
lived in a cave, and the first church was built around it. His skull is
kept in the present building in a silver reliquary, and many believe it
has miraculous powers to heal the sick.

The complex is now a convent. It dates from 1773 and is a
simple construction of good appearance, with excellent gardens.
These are meticulously tended by the nuns and in summer are an
oasis of greenery and colour in the barren landscape.

✚ 8E ✉ Near the village of Politikon ⊛ Group visits only: Mon, Tue, Thu
9–12 ✋ Free 🍴 Café opposite (£)

ASINOU CHURCH (PANAGIA FORVIOTISSA)

The fame of this church is such that it is quite a surprise to find it
so tiny, hidden on a north-facing hillside of eucalyptus and pine
trees. A steep clay-tiled outer roof protects the vulnerable
Byzantine dome and treasures within.

Asinou remains unscathed after 900 years. The frescoes are the
best of Cyprus's painted churches, the earliest dating back to the
12th century. They were added to over the years and culminate in
the powerful work by refugee painters from Asia Minor.

Christ is depicted in the sanctuary and the dome of the narthex,
gazing down. All around, the rank and file are beautifully illustrated.

✚ 6E ✉ Near Nikitari ⊛ Summer daily 9–5; winter 9–4; ask in Nikitari for
the priest with the key ✋ Free

KAKOPETRIA

This village stands high in the poplar-lined Solea Valley. As hill
villages go, it is quite large and is a popular holiday resort of
Cypriots. It is certainly not a smart place, the buildings are
generally old or ramshackle or both, but it has charm and many
traditional dwellings are being restored.

Up the valley (3km/2 miles) is the celebrated church of **Agios Nikolaos tis Stegis** with its famous roof. Below the town, at Galata, are the tiny churches of Panagia Eleousa and Panagia Theotokos, looking like country barns, with their roofs nearly touching the ground.

➕ 6D

Agios Nikolaos tis Stegis
🕓 Tue–Sat 9–4, Sun 11–4 💲 Free 🍴 Several cafés (£–££)

KYKKOS MONASTERY
See pages 42–43.

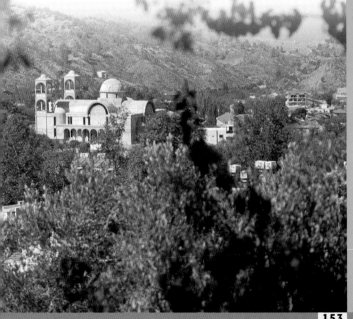

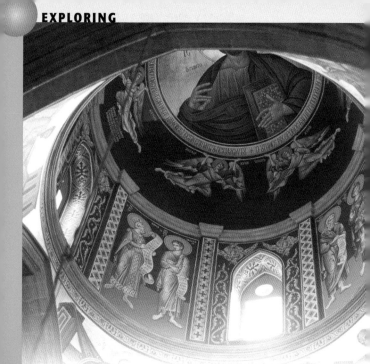

MACHAIRAS MONASTERY

The monastery was founded in the 12th century and grew around an icon of the Virgin Mary. Successive fires destroyed the original church and its wall paintings and in 1892 the entire monastery was burned to the ground.

The present building dates from the early 20th century, and its elevations are fortress-like, broken up with wooden balconies. Within is an impressive iconostasis, illuminated by chandeliers. On feast days rituals take place starting early and culminating at midnight with the abbot emerging with the holy fire, a glowing candle.

Outside a track leads down the wooded valley to the cave of Grigoris Afxentiou, second in command of EOKA during the uprising against the British. In 1957 a shepherd betrayed him and

British soldiers surrounded the cave entrance. Afxentiou chose to fight, dying eight hours later in his hideout.

✚ 8D ✉ Near Fikardou, eastern Troodos ⏱ Group visits only: Mon, Tue, Thu 9–12 ✋ Free 🍴 Cafés nearby (£)

MOUNT OLYMPOS

At 1,951m (6,399ft) above sea level, the summit of Mount Olympos is the highest ground in Cyprus. It is not an inaccessible peak, as a narrow road winds towards the top, stopping just below the summit at an unappealing radar dome and other military facilities. As a mountain it is thereby compromised, with no chance of proceeding higher to experience the view. This is reserved for those on the other, more inaccessible, side of the hill. In winter it is an unforgettable experience to stand in deep snow, bathed in sunlight, and look over to Morfou Bay and the Taurus Mountains of Turkey beyond.

✚ 5D ✉ 55km (34 miles) from Limassol, 97km (60 miles) from Nicosia
🍴 Cafés in Troodos village 4km (2.5 miles) away (£)

a drive into the Troodos Mountains

For Pafos visitors, the drive proper starts 17km (10.5 miles) towards Limassol. On the motorway, take the Mandria exit

Turn left at the Xeros River for Nikokleia, Mamonia and Agios Georgios. It is a splendid 55km (34 miles) up to Platres (Pano), through orchards and farmland.

The route from Limassol begins about 13km (8 miles) to the west, immediately after Erimi. Motorway drivers should use the Kantou exit.

Take the road north to Kantou, Souni and Agios Amvrosios. About 37km (23 miles) of pleasant uphill driving leads to Omodos village, now a popular tourist attraction. It is another 14km (8.5 miles) to meet up with the Pafos travellers at Platres.

Traverse the confusing streets of Platres to reach the Nicosia–Limassol highway and go left up to Troodos village – about 7km (4 miles). The route runs for 11km (7 miles) along the minor road to Prodromos, the highest village in Cyprus.

Soon after Prodromos the descent becomes dramatic, as the road twists and turns above the abyss.

This is a cherry-growing area, and its main villages – Pedoulas, Moutoullas and Kalopanagiotis – are reached in succession. Moutoullas is also famous for its spring water. After the excitement of the hairpin bends, it is a

simple run of about 8km (5 miles) before sweeping east
towards Linou and the Limassol–Nicosia highway.

*Turn right for Troodos/Limassol and climb the mountain.
Kakopetria (▶ 152–153), after 14km (8.5 miles), is
worth the detour. At Troodos village, Limassol-bound
drivers continue for 55km (34 miles), via Trimiklini and
Pano Polemedia. For Pafos turn off at Platres to reverse
the route via Mandria, Agios Nikolaos and Mamonia.*

Distance Limassol – 200km (124 miles); Pafos – 220km (136 miles)
Time 5–8 hours
Start/end point Limassol or Pafos ✚ 7B or 2C
Lunch Caruralli ✉ Pedoulas ☎ 2295 2441

PANAGIA TOU ARAKA

The paintings in this church are marvellous. Unfortunately the drive to get there is long and tiring, albeit through superb scenery. Should the church be locked, admission is then by courtesy of the priest, normally found in the village of Lagoudera.

The church retains the most complete series of wall paintings of the Byzantine period on the island and they have been restored, courtesy of UNESCO. They represent the metropolitan classicizing school in full bloom. Even visitors who know little of this Byzantine style will surely appreciate their magnificence.

✚ 6D ✉ Lagoudera 🕐 Daily 10–4 ✋ Free 🍴 Café in nearby village (£)

HOTELS

GREEK CYPRIOT NICOSIA (LEFKOSIA)
Averof (£)
Traditional hotel in a quiet area just outside the city.
✉ 19 Odos Averof, Nicosia ☎ 2277 3447; www.averof.com.cy

Classic (££)
Just within the walled city and convenient for the centre.
✉ 94 Odos Rigainis, Nicosia ☎ 2266 4006; www.classic.com.cy

Cleopatra (££)
In the new town with luxurious rooms. Pool and fine restaurant.
✉ 8 Odos Florinis, Nicosia ☎ 2284 4000; www.cleopatra.com.cy

Hilton Cyprus (£££)
See page 76.

TURKISH CYPRIOT NICOSIA (LEFKOŞA)
Royal (££)
Modern hotel with extensive facilities. Indoor pool.
✉ 19 Kemal Asik Caddesi ☎ 228 7621

Saray (££)
Central location and high standards make this a popular choice.
✉ Atatürk Meydanı ☎ 228 3115

AGROS
Rodon (££)
Modern hotel with 155 rooms offering mountain views. Outdoor pool. The restaurant is good.
✉ 1 Odos Rodou ☎ 2551 1201; www.rodonhotel.com

KAKOPETRIA
Hellas (££)
A 30-room hotel with comfortable rooms in the mountains.
✉ 20 Odos Mammantos ☎ 2292 2450

Linos Inn (££)
See pages 76–77.

PEDOULAS
Churchill Pinewood Valley (££)
Cosy 49-room hotel close to Prodromos, Cyprus's highest village.
✉ Prodromos–Pedoulas road ☎ 2295 2211

PLATRES
Forest Park (£££)
Set among pine and cedar trees. Facilities include pools and riding.
✉ 62 Odos Kalidonios ☎ 2542 1751; www.forestparkhotel.com.cy

RESTAURANTS

GREEK CYPRIOT NICOSIA (LEFKOSIA)
Abu Faysal (££)
Sophisticated Lebanese cuisine served in an elegant villa setting.
✉ 31 Odos Klimentou ☎ 2276 0353 ◑ Tue–Sun

Erodos (££)
In the old city by the Omeriye mosque, this is a reminder of an older Cyprus. There is Cypriot food and occasional Greek music.
✉ 11 Odos Patriarchou Grigoriou ☎ 2275 2250 ◑ Daily

Hippopotamus Grill (££)
International fare in attractive modern interior.
✉ 1 Leoforos Stassinou ☎ 2266 6305 ◑ Daily

Peri Orexeos (££)
The full Greek Cypriot experience, city style. Note the brown paper table coverings and unusual floor finish.
✉ 4–6 Odos Themistokli Dervi ☎ 2268 0608 ◑ Daily

Rimi (££)
This restaurant caters for the many visitors to the restored section of the old city and serves popular Cypriot and international dishes.
✉ 5 Odos Solonos, Laïki Geitonia ☎ 2268 0101 ◑ Daily

Sitio (££)

Watch the world go by from this café/restaurant. International dishes with a Mediterranean touch.

✉ 43 Leoforos Archiepiskopou Makariou III (at Odos Iras) ☎ 2245 8610 🕐 Daily

Xefoto (££)

This Laïki Geitonia café-restaurant sets itself apart from the run of traditional eateries in the area. The Cypriot and Mediterranean food complements this attitude by being more experimental.

✉ 6 Odos Aeschylou ☎ 2266 6567 🕐 Daily

TURKISH CYPRIOT NICOSIA (LEFKOŞA)

Boghijalian (££)

A restaurant much frequented by the locals, who enjoy a cuisine which embraces the best Turkish dishes.

✉ Arapahemet ☎ 228 0700 🕐 Daily

Califorian Restaurant (££)

The chef is a master of grilled meat dishes.

✉ Dereböyu ☎ 227 6938 🕐 Daily

El Sabor Latino (££)

Continental-style restaurant serving Mediterranean dishes. One of Nicosia's 'in' places. with live piano music on Saturday nights.

✉ Selimiye Meydanı ☎ 228 8322 🕐 Daily

Kibris Ashevi (Cyprus Kitchen) (£)

Interior design includes a collection of traditional fixtures and fittings. The pot roast from the clay oven outside is very satisfactory but must be ordered well in advance.

✉ 39A Atatürk Caddesi ☎ 223 1751 🕐 Daily

Saricizmeli (£)

One of the best value restaurants in the capital. Select a composite meal from a multitude of trays.

✉ 174 Girne Caddesi ☎ 227 3782 🕐 Daily

Zir Locanta (£)

Small restaurant that serves consistently good local dishes.

✉ Istanbul Caddesi ☎ 714 3064 🕐 Daily, dinner only

KAKOPETRIA
Linos Inn (££)

In the conservation zone, this restaurant in the Linos hotel is rural in style with good traditional dishes.

✉ 34 Odos Palaias ☎ 2292 3161 🕐 Daily

OMODOS
Makrinari (££)

Cypriot dishes served inside or in the shady courtyard.

✉ Adjacent to Troodos-Limassol crossroads ☎ 2542 1511 🕐 Daily

PLATRES
To Anoi (££)

Family taverna serving local fare and with a magnificent view.

✉ Platres centre ☎ 2542 2900 🕐 Daily

Yiolandel (££)

The paint may be fading a little but the 30-dish Sunday buffet is excellent and the home-made cakes are delicious. Proprietors Akis and Nitsa give their guests a sincere welcome.

✉ 3B Leoforos Makariou, near Pendeli Hotel ☎ 2542 1720 🕐 Daily

TRIMIKLINI
John's Restaurant (££)

Good value with some wonderful home-made food.

✉ Trimiklini ☎ 2543 2212 🕐 Daily

SHOPPING

JEWELLERY
Metaxas Factory

Tour shows gold and diamond crafting. Some wholesale prices.

🕐 8 Odos Pombieas, Strovolos Industrial Area, Nicosia 🕐 Tours Mon–Fri 9–5.30, Sat 9–1

Stephanides Jewellers
Long-established; excellent contemporary designs.
⊕ 23 Leoforos Archiepiskopou Makariou III, Nicosia ☎ 2266 1778

SOUVENIRS, HANDICRAFTS AND LEATHER
Cyprus Corner
Large collection of brass and copperware, plus onyx pieces.
✉ Selimiye Meydanı, Nicosia ☎ 227 1519

Cyprus Handicraft Centre
This centre, along with those in other towns, promotes and sells Cypriot handicrafts.
✉ 186 Leoforos Athalassis, Nicosia ☎ 2230 5024

Laïki Geitonia
Refurbished, traffic-free tourist area of the walled city; craft shops.
✉ East of Plateia Eleftherias, Nicosia (walled city)

Leventis Museum Gift Shop
Reproductions of historical artefacts, including some jewellery.
✉ 17 Odos Ippokratous, Nicosia (walled city) ☎ 2267 1997

Michalias Studio
High-quality ceramic tile murals, street numbers, coasters.
✉ 33 Odos Lefkonos, Nicosia (walled city) ☎ 2275 3900

Omodos
The tourist trail now takes in Omodos and souvenir shops abound.

TRNC Handicrafts Cooperative Ltd.
Local crafts sponsored by the North Cyprus administration.
✉ 9 Evkaf Is Hani, Keryneia (Girne) Caddesi, Nicosia ☎ 227 1368

STORES AND ARCADES
Mehmet Akif Caddesi, Nicosia
Head for the centre of this long street to browse upmarket boutiques. Plenty of cheap and cheerful outlets are here too.

Arasta Sokağı, Nicosia
Small shops, good for fabrics and inexpensive jeans and jackets.

Capital Center, Nicosia
The first real shopping centre in Cyprus is still worth a look.
✉ Leoforos Archiepiskopou Makariou III, Nicosia

City Plaza
Good multi-level department store.
✉ Leoforos Archiepiskopou Makariou III, Nicosia

Debenhams
Two stores: the one on Odos Kritis houses separate retailers on the various floors. The shop on Odos Lidras has a roof restaurant.
✉ Central: 18 Odos Kritis. Ledra: 171–179 Odos Lidras, Nicosia

ENTERTAINMENT AND SPORT

THEATRE AND CULTURAL EVENTS
British Council
Various cultural events in English.
✉ 3 Leoforos Mouseiou, Nicosia ☎ 2258 5000

Municipal Theatre
Regular performances by local and international companies.
✉ 4 Leoforos Mouseiou, Nicosia ☎ 2249 2900

HORSE-BACK RIDING
Nicosia Riding Club
Riding on summer days at Troodos Square on Mount Olympos.
✉ Lythrodontas, 15km (9 miles) south of Nicosia ☎ 9967 1789

SKIING
Mount Olympos
Season is January to March. Hire ski equipment in Sun Valley.

Cyprus Ski Club
✉ PO Box 22185, 1518 Nicosia ☎ 2267 5340

The North

This is the Turkish-controlled part of Cyprus, underpopulated compared to the remainder of the island. Change has been slow in coming, perhaps

due to the easy-going temperament of the Turkish Cypriots, but since the opening of the border in 2003 the pace has been steadily picking up.

Whatever the objectives of trade embargoes on this area they cannot detract from the magnificent scenery, and they have, to a diminishing extent, held back destructive mass tourism.

Along the north shore the spectacular Pentadaktylos (Beşparmak) Mountains run unbroken for 90km (56 miles). To the south the land is flat, opening out into the Mesaoria east of Nicosia. In summer it is impressively barren: in spring the colour has to be seen to be believed.

The narrow Karpasia peninsula is spectacular, with the blue Mediterranean visible to north and south.

Famagusta (Gazimağusa)

The city is divided, although not between Greek Cypriot and Turkish Cypriot. Varosha, the new town, with its painted hotels bordering the sandy beach, is closed to all but the military, as it has been since 1974. Visitors concentrate on the walled city. They are adequately compensated in that it is one of the finest surviving examples of medieval military architecture.

To pass through the massive walls is to pass through history, from the time of the Lusignans, Genoese and Venetians to the bloody siege by the Turks in 1570–71. They stormed the walls and all Cyprus was theirs for over 300 years.

In the narrow streets shops are unchanged by time or fashion. Dark interiors hide a miscellany of goods. The town can be a bustling place of noise and activity, but more often it is calm. They may not be as outgoing as their Greek Cypriot countrymen in the south, but Turkish Cypriots are equally courteous and helpful.

There is much unexpected open space in all directions: a chaotic panorama of unkempt gardens and scrubland, where palm trees shade ancient domed churches. Crumbling medieval buildings are all around. The battered minaret and massive buttress of Lala Mustafa Paşa Mosque form an impressive landmark.

✚ 20H

LALA MUSTAFA PAŞA MOSQUE

The building has been a mosque for over 400 years, but, the architecture is of a Gothic cathedral. There is a single minaret, well executed but certainly out of place. Even so, you can still admire the splendid six-light window of the west front. Three portals lead to the impressive interior, where Moslem simplicity has allowed the fine nave to survive the loss of its Christian decoration.

Lala Mustafa was the victorious commander of the Ottoman Turks when they broke into Famagusta in 1571. Surprisingly, the

mosque only received his name in 1954, before which it was called the Mosque of Santa Sophia.

✉ Naim Efendi Sokağı 🕐 Daily ✋ Free 🍴 Café opposite west front (£)

ST GEORGE OF THE GREEKS

This is a substantial church, though it has deteriorated significantly (it was built in 1359). The three apses are semicircular. A dome covered the middle section of the church, but by all accounts it collapsed under cannon fire in 1571. Some wall paintings survive, the best being in the eastern apse.

✉ Mustafa Ersu Sokağı 🕐 Daily ✋ Free

a walk around Famagusta (Gazimağusa)

The walk starts at the Land Gate entrance of the historic walled city.

Istiklal Caddesi is directly opposite and should be followed, taking care not to lose it at the three-way junction after 130m (142yds).

About 130m (142yds) farther, on the left, is the church of St Peter and St Paul (➤ 170).

A right turn along Sinan Paşa Sokağı leads to the Palazzo del Provveditore (Venetian Palace).

From here it is a short distance to Namık Kemal Meydanı, overlooked by the magnificent west front of Lala Mustafa Paşa Mosque (➤ 166).

A short retreat (to the west) picks up Kısla Sokağı, and in 130m (142yds) are the twin churches (now restored) of the Knights Templar and Knights Hospitaller. Immediately beyond the churches the road turns right, to the northeast, and in 120m (130yds) Cafer Paşa Sokagı.

At the eastern end are the ruined, but impressive buttresses and lancet windows of St George of the Latins. The Citadel (Othello's Tower), a short distance to the north, should not be missed.

The walk continues alongside the sea wall, down Canbulat Yolu, to reach the splendid Sea Gate after 200m (220yds).

In another 160m (175yds), a
short detour along Mustafa
Ersu Sokağı brings you to
the substantial church of St
George of the Greeks
(➤ 167). Returning to the
main road, the Canbulat
Museum is reached in
300m (327yds).

*The return to the Land
Gate is about 1,100m (just
over half a mile). Pass
outside the walls at the
Canbulat Museum and
follow the south wall.*

Distance 2.75km (1.7 miles)
Time 1–3.5 hours
Start/end point Land Gate
Lunch Café opposite west
front of Lala Mustafa Paşa
Mosque (£)

ST PETER AND ST PAUL
(SINAN PAŞA MOSQUE)

This Gothic church is distinctive for its spectacular flying buttresses. It was subsequently used as a mosque, as the ruined minaret in one corner testifies, and has also served as the municipal library. At other times it stored potatoes and grain and was known as the wheat mosque. On entering, the reason for the massive buttresses is apparent – the nave is of tremendous height, exerting a colossal force on the outside walls.

✉ Abdullah Paşa Sokağı ⏰ Jun–Sep Mon–Fri 9–2; Oct–May Mon–Fri 9–1, 2–4.45 ✋ Inexpensive 🍴 Cafés nearby (£)

VENETIAN WALLS

The original plan of the town was laid out by the Lusignans, but, when the Venetians took over in 1489 they completely renovated the enclosing walls. Experts in military architecture, they lowered the walls but increased the thickness, taking out all features that were vulnerable to cannon fire.

Any tour of the fortifications should take into account the great heat of summer and the low parapets everywhere.

The Citadel should be visited. It is also known as Othello's Tower, a name derived from Shakespeare's play, set in 'Cyprus. A seaport' and 'Cyprus. The Citadel'. Four great cylindrical towers guard the corners of the Citadel, and the carving over the entrance is an impressive winged lion of St Mark. The great hall is a massive vaulted chamber.

Taking a clockwise circuit of the walls, the Sea Gate, 200m (218yds) southeast, is the next place of interest. The gate's portcullis is part of the original Venetian work. In another 500m (545yds) is the Canbulat Gate and bastion (Canbulat was a Turkish hero of the siege), now a museum. Muskets and swords are displayed next to period dresses finished with fine embroidery.

Three bastions on the south wall lead to the Land Gate, the main entrance to the town. It is part of the Ravelin, a bastion considered impregnable when built, but later found wanting as its ditch offered cover to the enemy.

🕓 Citadel and Museum: Jun–Sep daily 9–7; Oct–May 9–1, 2–4.45 🎫 Citadel: moderate. Museum: inexpensive 🍴 Cafés nearby (£)

What to See in The North

BELAPAIS ABBEY

The setting of the abbey on the northern slopes of the Pentadaktylos (Beşparmak) Mountains is marvellous. Far below are almond and olive groves on the coastal plain, and Keryneia (Girne) seen to the west. Augustinian canons founded the abbey at the end of the 12th century, its importance lasting for some 300 years. Substantial parts collapsed long ago. The cloister is half ruined and flamboyant tracery hangs down from the pointed arches. On the north side

is the refectory, where the vault appears to spring lightly from the supporting capitals. Six tall windows look out on to the northern shore, and there is an exquisite pulpit, reached by an intricate stair constructed in the thickness of the wall. The 13th-century church is generally locked, but the custodian may open it on request.

In 1995 forest fires swept through the Pentadaktylos Mountains, advancing rapidly on Belapais (Beylerbeyi), the village where the author Lawrence Durrell lived from 1953 to 1956. In his celebrated *Bitter Lemons* he had written 'two things spread quickly; gossip and a forest fire'. It was only good fortune and the skill of the firefighters that prevented the destruction of Beylerbeyi in July 1995.

➕ 16K ✉ Belapais (Beylerbeyi) village 🕓 Jun–Sep daily 9–7; Oct–May daily 9–1, 2–4.45 🚻 Moderate 🍴 Café at the gate (£)

KANTARA

Kantara is the most easterly of the great Lusignan fortresses of the northern shore. At 600m (1,968ft) above sea level, its walls crown rocky crags, with the north shore way below.

The location at the eastern end of the Pentadaktylos (Beşparmak) Mountains gave the garrison control of the Karpasia peninsula. Visitors can, in a brief panorama, survey this unique landscape in its entirety.

Most of the castle is a ruin, although the formidable outer wall is substantially intact. Entrance is gained through a ruined barbican and two towers. Steps lead on to vaulted chambers and medieval latrines. On the highest ground, only a Gothic window remains.

🕂 20L 🖂 Near Kantara village 🕓 Jun–Sep daily 10–5; Oct–May daily 9–1, 2–4.45 ✋ Moderate 🍴 Cafés in Kantara village (£)

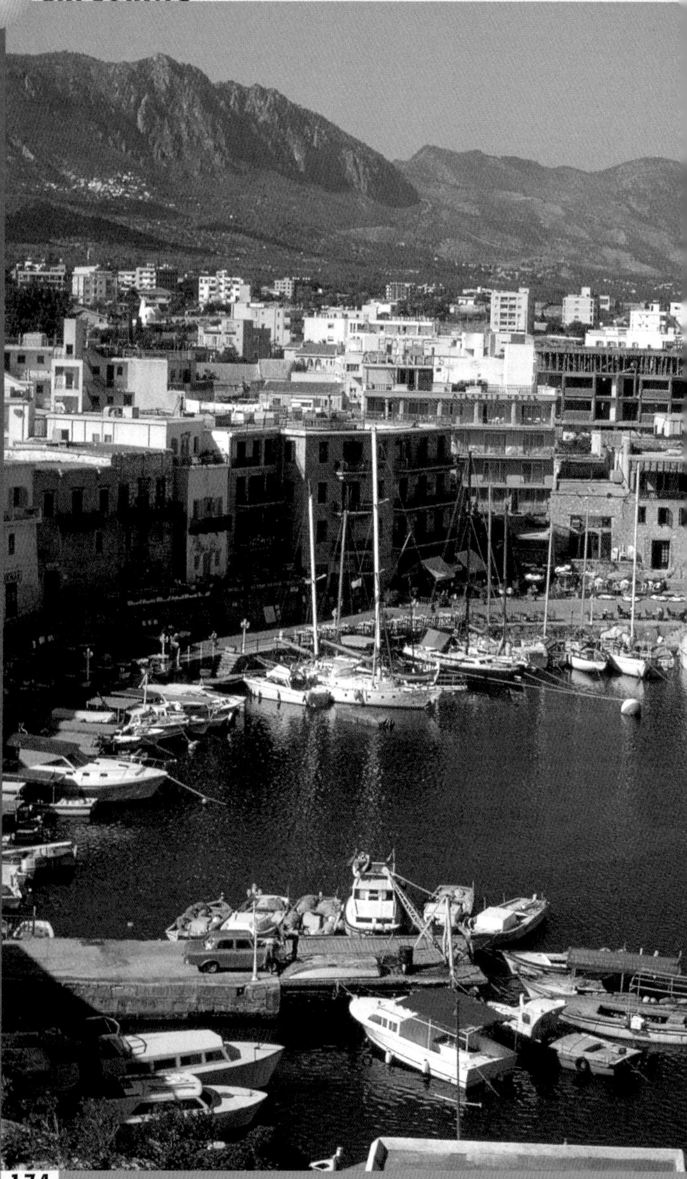

KERYNEIA (GIRNE)

Keryneia is unmatched in the rest of Cyprus. This is all
to do with the harbour and its magnificent setting.
Certainly the old buildings of the quayside, with the
exception of the customs houses, have all been
reconstituted as restaurants and bars, nevertheless
everything seems just perfect, day or night.

A huge cylindrical bastion from Venetian times forms
the east end of the harbour, a minaret rises up in the
middle ground and the bell-tower of the former
Archangelos Michaïl church, now an icon museum, is
in the west. Mountain ridges and summits run
unbroken into the hazy distance.

The origins of the **castle** are Lusignan, but it was the
Venetians who made it impregnable (and then
surrendered it to the Turks without a fight in 1570).
Inside, sunlight streams down from hidden windows
and openings. Entry into the complex structure is over
the moat, now dry, to reach a gatehouse. Progress is
then up a ramp, passing a small Byzantine chapel and
continuing to the northwest tower, where there is the
tomb of Sadık Paşa, killed in 1570. Various routes can
be taken to complete a tour of the castle, but care is
needed to keep clear of the unguarded drops.

The shipwreck museum within the castle is a
highlight. It houses the remains of a Hellenistic-era
merchant ship, raised from the seabed between 1968
and 1969. The blackened hull, astonishingly well
preserved, is more than 2,300 years old.

✚ 16K 🍴 Cafés around the harbour (£–££)

Keryneia Castle

✉ Harbour 🕐 Jun–Sep daily 9–7; Oct–May daily 9–1, 2–4.45
✋ Expensive

ST HILARION CASTLE
See pages 50–51.

SALAMIS
See pages 52–53.

SOLOI (SOLI)
The founders of Soli came from Greece and they created a city destined to play a major role in the struggle against Persian rule in the 5th and 4th centuries BC. However, only the later work of the Romans survives. They cut a theatre out of a rocky hillside overlooking Morfou Bay; today, most of this substantial work is a reconstruction. Near the road are the remains of a colonnade leading to an agora. Some mosaics remain, the bird representations being most impressive.

The wealth of Soli lay with its copper, mined from the surrounding hills. Boats from the city's harbour, long silted up, carried the metal to various parts of the Mediterranean.

➕ 5F ✉ Near Gemikonağı
🕐 Jun–Sep daily 9–7; Oct–May daily 9–1, 2–4.45 💷 Moderate

VOUNI

The road to ruined Vouni Palace spirals spectacularly upwards, a splendid area where the Troodos Mountains meet the northern shore. A series of terraces, swept bare by time, climb the hillside. The palace was clearly a substantial construction, with apartments, baths and courtyards. It was built in the 5th century BC by a pro-Persian king from Marion, possibly to counter the power of nearby Soli, a city loyal to the Greeks. The baths have a water system comparable to those of the Romans, but it is centuries earlier. At the top of the hill are the ruins of the Greek-style Temple of Athena.

✚ 5F ✉ Near Gemikonağı ✪ Jun–Sep daily 10–5; Oct–May daily 9–1, 2–4.45 ✋ Moderate

HOTELS

BELAPAIS (BEYLERBEYI) AREA

Altinkaya and Armonia (£)

A family-run place with 42 single-storey buildings near a swimming pool. The on-site restaurant is popular.

✉ Kazafani (Ozanköy) ☎ 815 5001

Ambelia Village (££)

An apartment complex that stands high above the village of Belapais (Beylerbeyi).

✉ Belapais–Kato Dhikomo road ☎ 815 3655

Belapais Gardens (££)

The luxury villa complex here lies among lemon trees near the ruined abbey.

✉ Keryneia–Belapais road ☎ 815 6066

FAMAGUSTA (GAZIMAĞUSA) AREA

Blue Sea (£)

This hotel by the sea is ideal for an overnight stay in Karpasia. Simple rooms. The fish dinner is excellent.

✉ 5km (3 miles) southeast of Dipkarpaz ☎ 372 2393

Mimoza (££)

Located at the water's edge on a sandy beach, near ancient Salamis.

✉ Just north of Salamis ☎ 378 8219

Palm Beach (£££)

Stylish hotel that stands out on the seafront thanks to its pink exterior. A casino and pool are among its entertainments. One of its aspects overlooks a rather derelict area.

✉ Leoforos Havva Sentürk ☎ 366 2000

Portofino (£)

Family-run hotel near the old town. Lots of facilities.

✉ Fevzi Çakmak Bulvarı ☎ 366 4392

Salamis Bay Conti Resort (£££)

Large impressive complex on a fine beach and close to the ruins of ancient Salamis. All the facilities you would expect of a 5-star hotel.

✉ Salamis Bay ☎ 378 8200; www.salamisbayconti.com

KERYNEIA (GIRNE) AND THE WEST
British (£)

Good Keryneia harbour location. There are great views from the restaurant and roof terrace. Ask about the VIP service.

✉ Kordonboyu, west end of harbour, Keryneia ☎ 815 2240; www.britishhotelcyprus.com

Bristol (£)

Good value accommodation. Good Turkish restaurant.

✉ Leoforos Hürriyet ☎ 815 6570

Courtyard Inn (£)

This small pension with a pool also has a good restaurant.

✉ Karakum ☎ 815 3343

Dome (££)

The longest established hotel in Cyprus occupies a prime position on a rocky outcrop near the harbour. A seawater swimming pool is built into a rocky enclosure to the front of the hotel.

✉ Kordonboyu, Keryneia ☎ 815 2453; www.domehotelcyprus.com

Dorana (£)

Within an easy walk of the shopping area and harbour, but having a peaceful feel.

✉ 143 Ziya Riski Caddesi, west of the harbour, Keryneia ☎ 815 3521

Grand Rock (£££)

Centrally located, efficient hotel.

✉ Kordonboyu ☎ 815 2238

LA Hotel (££)

Low-rise hotel around a good size pool. A pleasant beach is close
by, reached through an underpass to avoid crossing the road.

✉ Lapta, west of Keryneia ☎ 821 8981

Pia Bella (££)

About a 20-minute walk to the harbour. The garden annexe has
additional and superior rooms.

✉ 14 Iskendurun Caddesi Keryneia ☎ 815 5321

Soli Inn (£)

Seaside hotel near the ruins of Soli, in Güzelyurt Bay.

✉ Gemikonağı ☎ 727 7575

RESTAURANTS

AGIOS EPIKTITOS (ÇATALKÖY)
Lemon Tree (££)

A country house restaurant serving excellent seafood.

✉ Keryneia–Agios Epiktitos road ☎ 824 4045 ③ Daily

Mardin (££)

A seafood restaurant that is popular with locals.

✉ South edge of the village ☎ 824 4027 ③ Daily

FAMAGUSTA (GAZIMAĞUSA) AREA
Akdeniz (£)

Lively and popular with the locals, this roadside restaurant has a
wide, shady terrace. The seafood is delicious.

✉ Just north of Salamis Bay Hotel ☎ 378 8227 ③ Daily

Cyprus Gardens (£)

The restaurant's reputation derives from its excellent seafood and
chicken menu.

✉ Cyprus Gardens Complex, Boğaz ③ Daily

Cyprus House (££)

This old village house is decorated in 1930s style. Don't miss the mouth-watering local delicacies. Advisable to book.

✉ Polat Paşa Bulvarı, Famagusta, opposite post office ☎ 366 4845
🕐 Lunch and dinner; closed Sun

Mr Li's (£)

The Long Beach Country Club is an exclusive establishment in a superb setting by the beach. Mr Li serves Chinese and Malaysian food here in lavish surroundings.

✉ Long Beach Country Club, Yeni Iskele ☎ 378 8282 🕐 Daily noon–midnight

GÜZELYURT (MORFOU) AREA

Iskele (££)

Seafood and vegetable *meze*. Live music at the weekends.

✉ Güzelyurt town centre ☎ 714 2099 🕐 Daily

Liman Fish and Chips (£)

With a simple menu, this restaurant claims to be the best for fish in Cyprus. It is certainly a contender.

✉ Gemikonağı, near Lefka ☎ 727 7579 🕐 Daily

Şah's (££)

Kebab and excellent *meze*. Live music some nights.

✉ Güzelyurt, next to roundabout at entrance to town, arriving from north coast ☎ 714 3064 🕐 Daily

KERYNEIA (GIRNE) AND SURROUNDING AREA

Altınkaya 1 (££)

Popular with locals, its sits atop the cliffs overlooking a scenic stretch of coastline. Renowned for its fish dishes.

✉ Alsancak, 8km (5 miles) west of Keryneia ☎ 815 834 🕐 Thu–Tue

Altınkaya 2 (££)

A rich variety of seafood plus Turkish and English dishes.

✉ Osanköy, towards Beylerbeyi (Belapais) ☎ 815 500 🕐 Lunch and dinner

The Ambiance (££)
A la carte cuisine or 'full kebab' in a stunning seashore setting.
✉ Signposted off the main Keryneia–Lapithos (Girne–Lapta) road at Karaoğlanoğlu ☎ 822 2849 🕔 Daily

Benöz (£)
Family-run restaurant in a tranquil setting, serving simple but excellent Turkish cuisine and snacks.
✉ Alagadi, east of Keryneia ☎ 863 3823 🕔 Daily

Courtyard Inn (££)
This popular restaurant, with its country pub atmosphere, is run by expatriates from the UK. Try the spinach and apricot borek with the speciality fillet stuffed with pâté and prawns. Also open for bar snacks, and the roast on Sunday is good value.
✉ Karakum village, about 2km (1 mile) east of Keryneia ☎ 815 3343 🕔 Daily

Crows Nest (££)
Pub and restaurant that caters for visitors and the villagers. Cosy atmosphere and open plan kitchen. The menu embraces Turkish and continental cuisine.
✉ Karaman ☎ 822 2567 🕔 Daily

Efendi's House (££)
This is an intimate restaurant tucked away in the Keryneia back streets. It is popular and reservation is advisable if you'd like to sample the Cypriot and French cuisine.
✉ 6 Kamil Paşa Road, Keryneia ☎ 815 1149 🕔 Daily 11.30–2.30, 7.30–10

Guler's Fish Restaurant (££)
Well sited overlooking a cove by the shore. Many of the locals claim that the best fish in Keryneia is served here.
✉ Keryneia, to the west by the Serif Hotel Apartments ☎ 822 2718 🕔 Daily

Harbour Club (£££)

Splendid view over the harbour. French cuisine, first-class seafood and many typical Turkish dishes.

✉ Harbour (near castle), Keryneia ☎ 815 2211 🕐 Daily

Harbour Taverna (££)

Weekend nights are traditional taverna-style with live entertainment plus *meze* and kebabs.

✉ Kordonboyu ☎ 815 5344 🕐 Daily

Hensons (££)

Very good fresh fish. The special is the charcoal grilled steak.

✉ Alsancak, on the road to Deniz Kizi Hotel ☎ 821 2890 🕐 Daily

The Hideaway Club (££)

International dishes in a poolside restaurant. The mountain views are breathtaking.

✉ Trimithi–Karmi road ☎ 822 2620 🕐 Daily

Hilarion Village Restaurant (££)

Tasty local dishes on the rarefied heights of the Keryneia hills.

✉ Karmi ☎ 822 2574 🕐 Daily

Jashan (£££)

Indian cuisine and excellent service. Booking is advisable.

✉ Keryneia–Lapithos (Girne–Lapta) road 🕐 Daily

Le Jardin (£££)

Fine cuisine in romantic setting with bar. One of its features is the pretty garden, as the name suggests, complete with running stream. Reservations are advisable.

✉ Karakum, east of Keryneia ☎ 824 4398 🕐 Closed Thu

Lemon Tree (££)

Excellent Turkish Cypriot menu including hot stuffed pastries, grilled fish and meat plus a good *meze*. Long-established

✉ Çatalköy road, 5km (3 miles) east of Keryneia ☎ 815 4045 🕐 Daily

Mountain House (££)

European and Turkish cuisine in an established family concern.

✉ Beylerbeyi (Belapais) road, Keryneia ☎ 815 3881 🕐 Mon–Sat lunch only; closed Sun

Niazi's (£)

This popular restaurant near Keryneia harbour serves excellent meat dishes; the cooking of kebabs has been turned into an art form.

✉ West of the harbour, opposite Dome Hotel, Keryneia ☎ 815 2160 🕐 Daily

The Old Mill (£)

Simple but tasty fare served in an eclectically decorated old olive mill.

✉ Central Ozanköy ☎ 815 6818 🕐 Thu–Tue dinner only

Padişah (£)

Traditional Turkish Cypriot fare served in an unpretentious setting.

✉ Central Keryneia, Bozkırlı Sokağı, opposite the Colony Hotel ☎ 815 9763 🕐 Mon–Sat

Rafters Pub and Bistro (££)

Snack and bistro menu to suit all appetites. Special requests cooked to order but notice required. Booking advisable.

✉ Ozanköy road, 4km (2.5 miles) east of Keryneia ☎ 815 2946 🕐 Tue–Sat 6–12, Sun 12–7

Set Italian Restaurant (££)

Courtyard setting with lovely trees. Perfect for a candlelit dinner.

✉ Caferpaşa, Keryneia, near mosque on first back street behind harbour ☎ 815 6008 🕐 Daily 6–11

Tree of Idleness (££)

Fish and kebab dishes and Turkish Cypriot *meze*. Live music Saturday. Courtesy shuttle to hotels in Keryneia. Some dispute the claim to host Durrell's famous tree, but it doesn't dampen the

enthusiasm of the many who pile in for Saturday 'Cyprus nights'.
✉ Beylerbeyi (Belapais) ☎ 815 3380 ⊕ Daily

Valley View Restaurant (££)
The menu is impressive, daily fresh fish and seafood, full kebab, chicken dishes, *meze* and others.
✉ Yani/Çatalköy ☎ 868 7070 ⊕ Daily

Veranda (££)
Seaside restaurant with a varied menu. Booking advisable.
✉ Sehit Ridvan Street, eastern end of Karaoğlanoğlu ☎ 822 2034
⊕ Tue–Sun

Yama Restaurant (££)
Over 30 kinds of *meze* are on offer along with fish specials.
✉ Kervansaray, Karaoğlanoğlu ☎ 822 2888 ⊕ Daily

Yenihan (££)
Popular place on the west side of Keryneia serving *mezes* and Turkish dishes. Cypriot nights with a bellydancer and live music.
✉ Keryneia–Lapithos (Girne–Lapta) road ☎ 815 8942 ⊕ Daily

LAPITHOS (LAPTA) AREA
Ali Paşa's (£)
Not a very attractive taverna, but the seafood dishes are good.
✉ Keryneia–Lapithos road ☎ 821 8942 ⊕ Thu–Tue

Shirley Valentine's (££)
Small restaurant on the seafront serving international dishes.
✉ Karavas (Alsancak) ☎ 821 8922 ⊕ Thu–Tue

SHOPPING

SOUVENIRS, HANDICRAFTS AND LEATHER
Bayramoglu Ltd.
Quality handbags and shoes.
✉ Hurriyet Sokağı, Keryneia (Girne) ☎ 815 2216

Ceramic Centre
Largest pottery showroom in the North.
✉ Ortaköy, 3km (2 miles) northwest of Nicosia ☎ 223 2302

Design 74
Traditional pottery made while you watch.
✉ Near Karaoğlanoğlu, 2.5km (1.5 miles) from Keryneia ☎ 815 2507

Senak Souvenir Shop
Interesting onyx and copper designs and local pottery plus carpets.
✉ Harbour by the mosque, Keryneia (Girne) ☎ 815 2811

JEWELLERY SHOPS
These can be found dotted about the streets of all the North's main towns, but a good place to shop around is on the main street of Keryneia (Girne), where several are found in a cluster around the crossroads leading down to the seafront promenade.

CULTURAL EVENTS
A variety of seminars and other cultural events in the North take place throughout the year. Contact the Atatürk Cultural Centre in Northern Nicosia for details.

SPORT

HORSE-BACK RIDING
Dortnal Riding Club
✉ Karaoğlanoğlu ☎ 822 2293

Riverside HV Horse Riding
✉ Karaoğlanoğlu ☎ 8222 2293

Tunac Riding Club
✉ Karaoğlanoğlu ☎ 822 2868

Index

Acknowledgements

The Automobile Association would like to thank the following photographers, companies and picture libraries for their assistance in the preparation of this book.

Abbreviations for the picture credits are as follows: - (t) top; (b) bottom; (l) left; (r) right; (AA) AA World Travel Library.

4l Pano Panagia, AA/R Rainford; **4c** Larnaka Airport, AA/A Kouprianoff; **4r** Kyrenia, AA/A Kouprianoff; **5l** Petra tou Romiou, AA/M Birkitt; **5c** Lefkara, AA/S/L Day; **6/7** Pano Panagia, AA/R Rainford; **8/9** fishing nets, AA/A Kouprianoff; **10/1t** harbour Pafos, AA/A Kouprianoff; **10bl** Sanctuary of Apollo Hylates, AA/A Kouprianoff; **10br** man and donkey Pafos, AA/A Kouprianoff; **11** Ayios Theodhoros, AA/A Kouprianoff; **12** salad, AA/S Day; **13t** café Pafos harbour, AA/S Day; **13c** Cyprus Delights, AA/A Kouprianoff; **12/3** fishermen Larnaka, AA/S Day; **14** wines and spirits, Larnaka, AA/R Rainford; **14/5** shop keeper, AA/A Kouprianoff; **15** grapes, AA/A Kouprianoff; **16/7** Kourion, AA/M Birkitt; **17l** Famagusta beach, AA/A Kouprianoff; **17r** wedding Xylotymbou, AA/A Kouprianoff; **18** Artemis trail, AA/A Kouprianoff; **19** Mount Olympus, AA/S Day; **20/1** Larnaka airport, AA/A Kouprianoff; **24** Greek dancers, AA/M Birkitt; **26** car and motorbike rental, AA/M Birkitt; **27** signs, AA/A Kouprianoff; **28** tour bus, AA/A Kouprianoff; **29** taxi driver, AA/A Kouprianoff; **30** public telephone, AA/M Birkitt; **34/5** Kyrenia, AA/A Kouprianoff; **36** Akamas Peninsular, AA/S Day; **36/7** coastline Akamas Peninsular, AA/S Day; **37** walkers Akamas Peninsular, AA/S Day; **38** embroidery Mevlevi Tekke, AA/M Birkitt; **38/9** Salt Lake, AA/A Kouprianoff; **39** Hala Sultan Tekke Mosque, AA/S Day; **40** Kourion, AA/M Birkitt; **40/1** Kourion, AA/R Rainford; **41** amphitheatre Kourion, AA/M Birkitt; **42/3** Kykkos Monastery, AA/S Day; **43** painting Kykkos Monastery AA/A Kouprianoff; **44** petrol tank, AA/R Rainford; **44/5** Lara, AA/S Day; **45t,c** loggerhead turtles, Lara, AA/A Kouprianoff; **46/7** Venetian wall, Nicosia, S Day; **47t** Corner of Venetian Wall, AA/A Kouprianoff; **47b** Nicosia, AA/S Day; **48tl** mosaic House of Dionysos, AA/R Rainford; **48bl** Tombs of the Kings, AA/M Birkitt; **48/9** mosaic Pafos, AA/A Kouprianoff; **50** St Hilarion Castle, AA/A Kouprianoff; **50/1** St Hilarion Castle, AA/A Kouprianoff; **52** Salamis, AA/A Kouprianoff; **52/3** Salamis, AA/A Kouprianoff; **53** mosaic Salamis, AA/A Kouprianoff; **54** Troodos foothills, AA/S Day; **54/5** Kaledonia Falls, AA/A Kouprianoff; **55** lady fruit seller, AA/M Birkitt; **56/7** Petra tou Romiou, AA/M Birkitt; **58/9** café, Latsi, AA/A Kouprianoff; **60/1** lace, Lefkara, AA/A Kouprianoff; **62/3** Amathous, AA/S Day; **64/5** hang-glider, AA/A Kouprianoff; **66** children, Nicosia, AA/R Rainford; **68/9** Coral Bay, AA/S Day; **70/1** Lefkara, AA/M Birkitt; **72/3** Limassol, AA/A Kouprianoff; **73** Limassol, AA/M Birkitt; **74/5** Panagia Chrysorrogiatissa, AA/A Kouprianoff; **76/7** Hotel, Limassol, AA/A Kouprianoff; **78** Akamas Peninsular, AA/A Kouprianoff; **80/1** Turkish Nicosia, AA/A Kouprianoff; **82/3** Lefkara, AA/S Day; **85** Priest, AA/S Day; **86** Agios Lazaros church, AA/A Kouprianoff; **86/7** Larnaka, AA/M Birkitt; **88/9c** Pierides Museum, Larnaca, AA/A Kouprianoff; **88/9b** Kition, AA/M Birkitt; **89** Fort, Larnaka, AA/M Birkitt; **90** Agia Napa, AA/M Birkitt; **91** Hala Sultan Tekke, AA/A Kouprianoff; **92** Nissi Beach, AA/R Rainford; **92/3** Potamos, AA/S Day; **94/5** Stravrouni monastery, AA/R Rainford; **96** Stravrouni monastery, AA/A Kouprianoff; **103** Limassol, AA/M Birkitt; **105** Limassol, AA/M Birkitt; **106/7** Castle, Limassol, AA/M Birkitt; **107** Aphrodite of Soli, Cyprus Museum, AA/R Rainford; **108/9** Municipal Gardens, Limassol, AA/M Birkitt; **109** Akrotiri Peninsula, AA/A Kouprianoff; **110** Khirokitia, AA/M Birkitt; **111** Kolossi Castle, AA/A Kouprianoff; **112** Lefkara, AA/S Day; **112/3** Petra tou Romiou, AA/S Day; **114** Temple of Apollo Hylates, AA/A Kouprianoff; **121** Pafos, AA/M Birkitt; **122/3** Agia Solomoni, AA/A Kouprianoff; **124/5** Pafos, AA/M Birkitt; **125** St Paul's Pillar, AA/S Day; **126** Saranda Kolones, AA/S Day; **127** Tomb of the Kings, AA/M Birkitt; **128/9** Agios Neofytos monastery, AA/S Day; **130/1** Chrysorrogiatissa monastery, AA/A Kouprianoff; **131** Agia Paraskevi, AA/A Kouprianoff; **132/3** Palaia Pafos, AA/M Birkitt; **133** Pano Panagia, AA/M Birkitt; **134** Polis, AA/A Kouprianoff; **134/5** Pomos, AA/A Kouprianoff; **141** Nicosia, AA/R Rainford; **142** Archbishop Makarios statue, AA/S Day; **142/3** Agios Ionnis cathedral, AA/A Kouprianoff; **143** Agios Ionnis cathedral, AA/M Birkitt; **144** Cyprus museum, AA/R Rainford; **144/5** Cyprus museum, AA/A Kouprianoff; **145** Famagusta Gate, AA/M Birkitt; **146** Omeriye Mosque, AA/M Birkitt; **148** Buyuk Han, AA/R Bulmar; **148/9** Buyuk Han, AA/M Birkitt; **149** Turkish Cypriot lady, AA/M Birkitt; **150** Mevlevi Tekke, AA/A Kouprianoff; **151** Selimiye Mosque, AA/A Kouprianoff; **152/3** Kakopetria, AA/M Birkitt; **154/5** Machairas Monastery, AA/M Birkitt; **155** Artemis trail, AA/A Kouprianoff; **156/7** Pedoulas, AA/S Day; **158** Panagia Tou Araka, AA/A Kouprianoff; **165** Famagusta, AA/A Kouprianoff; **167** Lala Mustafa Pasa Mosque, AA/A Kouprianoff; **168/9** St George of the Latins, AA/A Kouprianoff; **169** Citadel, AA/R Bulmar; **170** St Peter and St Paul church, AA/A Kouprianoff; **170/1** Famagusta, AA/H Ulucam; **172** Bellapais Abbey, AA/A Kouprianoff; **173** Kantara castle, AA/R Bulmar; **174** Kyrenia, AA; **176/7** Soli, AA/H Ulucam; **178t** Vouni, AA; **178** Vouni, AA/A Kouprianoff.

Every effort has been made to trace the copyright holders, and we apologise in advance for any accidental errors. We would be happy to apply the corrections in the following edition of this publication.

Dear Reader

Your comments, opinions and recommendations are very important to us. So please help us to improve our travel guides by taking a few minutes to complete this simple questionnaire.

You do not need a stamp (unless posted outside the UK). If you do not want to cut this page from your guide, then photocopy it or write your answers on a plain sheet of paper.

Send to: **The Editor, AA World Travel Guides, FREEPOST SCE 4598, Basingstoke RG21 4GY.**

Your recommendations...

We always encourage readers' recommendations for restaurants, nightlife or shopping – if your recommendation is used in the next edition of the guide, we will send you a **FREE AA Guide** of your choice from this series. Please state below the establishment name, location and your reasons for recommending it.

_____
_____
_____
_____
_____
_____

Please send me **AA Guide** _____

About this guide...

Which title did you buy?

AA _____

Where did you buy it?_____

When? m m / y y

Why did you choose this guide? _____
_____
_____
_____
_____

Did this guide meet your expectations?

Exceeded ☐ Met all ☐ Met most ☐ Fell below ☐

Were there any aspects of this guide that you particularly liked? _____
_____
_____
_____

continued on next page...

Is there anything we could have done better? _____

_____

_____

_____

About you...

Name (*Mr/Mrs/Ms*) _____

Address _____

_____

_____ Postcode

Daytime tel nos _____

Email _____

Please only give us your mobile phone number or email if you wish to hear from us about other products and services from the AA and partners by text or mms, or email.

Which age group are you in?
Under 25 ☐   25–34 ☐   35–44 ☐   45–54 ☐   55–64 ☐   65+ ☐

How many trips do you make a year?
Less than one ☐   One ☐   Two ☐   Three or more ☐

Are you an AA member? Yes ☐   No ☐

About your trip...

When did you book? m m / y y   When did you travel? m m / y y

How long did you stay? _____

Was it for business or leisure? _____

Did you buy any other travel guides for your trip?

If yes, which ones? _____

_____

_____

Thank you for taking the time to complete this questionnaire. Please send it to us as soon as possible, and remember, you do not need a stamp (*unless posted outside the UK*).

AA Travel Insurance call 0800 072 4168 or visit www.theAA.com

---